CONTROVERSY!

Prisons

Jeff Burlingame

Marshall Cavendish
Benchmark
New York

With special thanks to Dr. Faye Taxman, director of the Center for Advancing Correctional Excellence at George Mason University, for reviewing the text of this book.

Copyright © 2012 Marshall Cavendish Corporation
Published by Marshall Cavendish Benchmark
An imprint of Marshall Cavendish Corporation

Other Marshall Cavendish Offices:
Marshall Cavendish International (Asia) Private Limited, 1 New Industrial Road, Singapore 536196 • Marshall Cavendish International (Thailand) Co Ltd. 253 Asoke, 12th Flr, Sukhumvit 21 Road, Klongtoey Nua, Wattana, Bangkok 10110, Thailand • Marshall Cavendish (Malaysia) Sdn Bhd, Times Subang, Lot 46, Subang Hi-Tech Industrial Park, Batu Tiga, 40000 Shah Alam, Selangor Darul Ehsan, Malaysia

Marshall Cavendish is a trademark of Times Publishing Limited.
All websites were available and accurate when this book was sent to press.

Library of Congress Cataloging-in-Publication Data
Burlingame, Jeff. • Prisons : rehabilitate or severely punish? / Jeff Burlingame.
p. cm.—(Controversy!) • Includes bibliographical references and index.
ISBN 978-1-60870-493-4 (print) • ISBN 978-1-60870-645-7 (ebook)
1. Prisons—United States—Juvenile literature. 2. Criminals—Rehabilitation—United States—Juvenile literature. I. Title. II. Series. • HV9471.B87 2012 • 365'.973--dc22 • 2010037184

Publisher: Michelle Bisson • Art Director: Anahid Hamparian
Series Designer: Alicia Mikles • Photo research by Lindsay Aveilhe

The photographs in this book are used by permission and through the courtesy of:
Cover photo by © Andrew Garn Photography; Bettmann/Corbis: p. 4; Grosvenor Prints/Mary Evans Picture Library: p. 8; The Granger Collection, NYC: p. 18; John Smierciak/MCT/Newscom: p. 21; MaxWhittaker/Picturemaxx/Redux: p. 29; Aurelia Ventura/LA Opinion/Newscom: p. 31; AP Photo: p. 36;The Florida Times-Union, Jon M. Fletcher/AP Photo: p. 37; Damian Dovarganes/AP Photo: p. 39; Zuma Press/Newscom: pp. 46, 53; John Smierciak/MCT/Newscom: p. 54; Darlene Prois/Zuma Press/Newscom: p. 56; Joe Amon/The Denver Post/AP Photo: p. 61; Nanine Hartzenbusch/AP Photo: p. 68; St. Louis Post Dispatch, HO/AP Photo: p. 71; Richard Sheinwald/AP Photo: p. 73; Robert Cooper/AP Photo: p. 82; Gregory Bull/AP Photo: p. 87; Stephen Mally/The New York Times/Redux: p. 94; Coutesy King Co. Prosecutor's Office, File/AP Photo: p. 97; Charles Osgood/ Chicago Tribune/MCT/Newscom: p. 99; Ralph Crane/Time Life Pictures/Getty Images: p. 108; Jake Schoellkopf/AP Photo: p. 114; Sally Ryan/The New York Times/Redux: p. 117.

Printed in Malaysia (T)
135642

Contents

The riot over poor living conditions at Attica State Prison in 1971 sparked a debate about how criminals should be treated that is still ongoing to this day.

Introduction

AS LONG AS THERE HAVE BEEN PRISONS THERE HAS
been debate as to exactly what role they should play in American
society. Should prisons be dark and uncaring places whose main
purpose is to isolate convicted criminals from the rest of society
and punish them for their unlawful deeds? Or should they primarily be dedicated to rehabilitation—that is, providing inmates treatment and educational opportunities that will allow violators the
opportunity to rejoin society and behave in a lawful and productive
manner once they do so? Today, hundreds of years after the first
prison opened its doors, the United States incarcerates more people
than any other country in the world. The debate as to how those
prisoners should be treated continues.

Though the principal job of early prisons was to punish criminals, reformers eventually began to change that mission. One way
they did so was by referring to prisons as correctional institutions,
a much softer term, suggesting a place of treatment rather than a
place of punishment. Other reforms followed. By the end of the
nineteenth century, a juvenile justice system had been created that
was dedicated to rehabilitating young offenders in reform schools.

But over the past forty years, the pendulum has again swung—
back toward where it was in the country's earliest days. For the most
part, prisons of today are focused on punishment and retribution.
The shift was due in large part to a rise in the violent crime rate

and a September 1971 incident that—thanks to the immediacy of television—alerted much of America to what life in prison really was like. The riot at Attica Correctional Facility in New York began with a prison uprising sparked by poor living conditions, and ended five days later following the deaths of thirty-two prisoners and eleven guards who had been taken hostage. The shift also was due to a public that thought that being in prison was not a big deal and was not that much of a punishment.

The Attica incident was the bloodiest prison battle in American history, and its impact extended far beyond the prison walls. A majority of Americans soon called for tougher laws that would put criminals behind bars for longer periods of time. Many of these criminals were drug users who swelled the inmate ranks. Subsequently, during the first decade of the twenty-first century, the United States has had the highest rate of incarceration of any country in the world. Supporters claim that lengthy prison sentences have cut down the rate of violent crime, which fell to historic lows in the 2000s. Others disagree, claiming that the lower crime rates were the result of better policing and better citizen management of behaviors such as drunk driving and leaving doors unlocked.

Meanwhile, as prisons overflow, state budgets are breaking under the weight of huge correctional expenditures. Reductions in expenditures have impacted conditions inside prisons, and there are debates over the quality of health care and vocational training, the levels of violence, the treatment of undocumented immigrants, and the treatment of juvenile offenders.

At one end of the spectrum, there are states trying to prevent more people from being incarcerated. They are turning to programs such as drug courts, which offer those convicted of drug offenses an alternative to prison—close monitoring by the court, and drug treatment. States have started to take a look at changing tough sentencing laws that keep convicted felons behind bars for long periods of time. Some states are providing increased opportunities for prisoners to receive higher education and job training so they will have a better chance of success once they are released. At the other end of the spectrum, there are those who believe reformation programs should not be offered at all and that the punishment of sitting behind bars is exactly what criminals need.

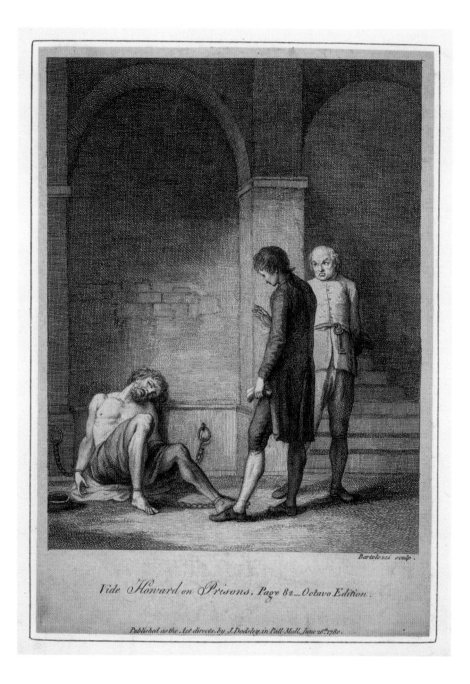

Vide *Howard* on *Prisons*, Page 82—Octavo Edition.

Bartolozzi sculp.

Published as the Act directs, by J.Dodsley, in Pall Mall, June 28. 1780.

Sheriff John Howard was appalled by the conditions he found in the British county jails, and that led him to advocate for, and help institute, major reforms.

1 History of U.S. Prisons

> The jail was nothing more than a dank, dismal cavern with one accessible entrance, down which a forty-foot ladder led to the depths from the guardhouse. Year-round the temperature below remained an uncomfortable fifty degrees or thereabouts; the only sound was the everlasting rhythmical drip of water, and the only light the daylight at the bottom of the well shaft, unless a prisoner cared to procure his own candles.

AS REPORTED BY WRITER W. STORRS LEE, SUCH WERE the conditions in the earliest days of Newgate Prison in Simsbury, Connecticut. The prison—located in an abandoned copper mine where British prisoners had been kept during the American Revolution—first opened its doors in 1773 as the colony's option for housing serious criminals, and became a state prison in 1790. Prisoners at Newgate were subjected to violence and poorly fed, and eventually staged the first prison riot in American history.

Although conditions faced by prisoners at Newgate may sound unusually harsh, they were not atypical for the time. Similar conditions had existed for centuries in European prisons, although that began to change shortly after Newgate came into existence.

Led by lecturer and reformer John Howard, a prison reform movement was underway in England. With Howard's help, the British had begun to recognize that prisoners might change their lives if they were treated more humanely. Howard saw prisons as places where criminals might do penance for their crimes, recognize their sinful ways, and reform. He used the word "penitentiary" to describe the type of prison he had in mind, and he wrote the Penitentiary Act, which subsequently was passed by the British Parliament in 1779. The act helped improve conditions for prisoners based on religious tenets, and focused on their rehabilitation in addition to their punishment.

Howard's reforms were put to the test in 1785, at a jail that opened at Wymondham in Norfolk, England. Instead of housing all prisoners together, as had been the norm, male and female criminals were confined separately at Wymondham. Prisoners also were placed in separate cells where they could have time to think about their crimes and do penance for them so they could transform their lives.

In the United States, Howard's reforms were adopted in 1790 in Philadelphia at the Walnut Street Jail. The jail used the "Pennsylvania" system of prison reform. Inmates were kept in solitary confinement in separate cells, where they were expected to read the Bible and repent for their crimes. At first, they were given nothing to do but those tasks, but gradually they were given work, such as shoemaking and chair making, to keep them busy. Since each prisoner worked, ate, and slept in his or her cell, the cells had to be fairly large, which meant each correctional institution could only house a small prison population. Western State Penitentiary, which opened in Pittsburgh, Pennsylvania, in 1826, also adopted this system, as did Eastern State Penitentiary, which opened in Philadelphia in 1829.

An alternative to the Pennsylvania system was initiated in 1821 at a prison in Auburn, New York. Under the "Auburn" system, prisoners slept in separate cells, but worked and ate together in large common rooms. In these areas, they were not permitted to talk to each other. At Auburn, long cell blocks with small individual cells were constructed, enabling each prison to house a larger population than under the Pennsylvania system. When prison authorities discovered that it was more efficient to have prisoners work together, and learned that they produced far more this way, the Auburn system gradually became the model for most U.S. prisons. Since the products produced by inmates could be sold outside the prison, the profits could be used to pay for much of the cost of running the correctional institutions they were made in. Prisoners were now helping to pay for their own upkeep.

New prisons based on the Auburn system soon sprang up. In the late 1820s, the Sing Sing prison opened in Ossining, New York. A year prior, the Wethersfield State Prison had opened in Wethersfield, Connecticut. Many other states soon opened prisons of their own. In fact, between 1825 and 1870, twenty-three prisons based on the Auburn system opened. Gradually, the system's rule of silence was ended, and prisoners were permitted to speak to each other.

Nevertheless, conditions inside the prisons remained harsh. Each prisoner wore a striped suit that identified him or her as a convicted felon. If prisoners did not follow the rules, they were severely disciplined. That could mean they were saddled with a ball and chain wrapped around their body to prevent escape and ease of movement, were whipped by prison guards, or were placed for many hours in pillories, wooden frames with holes for a prisoner's head and hands.

In some states, prisoners were regularly leased out to private contractors to do a variety of work. Shackled together in what was called a chain gang, they worked at building railroads, repairing roadways, or doing plantation work.

After the country's slaves were freed following the Civil War, African Americans still were not treated fairly. They often were treated badly and arrested if they were suspected of not having jobs or of committing a minor crime, such as fighting or petty theft. As stated in *The American Prison*, "Instead of being punished on plantations, former slaves were jammed into overcrowded, dilapidated correctional facilities." Many of them were sent out to farms where they picked cotton, cut sugarcane, and harvested vegetables. As such, the former slaves were right back to doing what they had done before they had been freed.

Prisoners were brought to plantations in mobile cages that housed up to thirty people. The former slaves worked long hours, with little to eat, and received severe punishment if they misbehaved. *The American Prison* states, "Humane treatment of prisoners . . . took a back seat to profit making."

Prison Reform

During the last quarter of the nineteenth century, a reform movement swept across the United States that affected many parts of American society, including state prisons. America's vast industrialization had created large manufacturing plants, enormous mining operations, and sprawling cities. Working conditions in the factories and mines often were dangerous, while in cities, hundreds of thousands of workers often lived in crowded and unsanitary slums. Also, large numbers of foreigners who had entered the cities in search of factory work had found none. Rather than retreating to their homelands of China, Ireland, and Italy, the jobless men remained in the cities and lived in the slums. Such areas became hotbeds for crime.

A group of reformers began to investigate these conditions and write about them in popular magazines. They also focused on the treatment of prisoners inside America's correctional institutions—including the harsh punishments meted out to prisoners, the inadequate food, and overcrowding.

During the remainder of the nineteenth century, more prisons continued to be built as the prison population increased. In 1850, there were thirty prisoners for every 100,000 Americans. By 1900, this number had more than doubled to 75 per 100,000.

Jail, Prison, Penitentiary

Understanding the various levels of the criminal justice system in America can be summed up with one key point: it's all a matter of degree.

In most places, criminal courts—and places to keep accused and convicted criminals—are set up at different levels that depend on the severity of the crime. Criminal courts are distinct from civil courts, which are set up to decide lawsuits.

District courts usually are the lowest level, and are associated with city jails. These will try the lowest and least severe crimes, from traffic offenses to shoplifting, and will sometimes try more severe crimes depending on where the crime was committed and the resources of the law enforcement agencies involved. This is because more severe crimes, such as rape and murder, require more expensive resources, such as laboratory work. Further, in cases where, for example, a murder has been committed in a smaller town, the larger county jurisdiction or even the state may try the case in order to cover the costs.

City jails will generally serve to keep convicted criminals whose sentences are less than thirty days, and also will be used to hold accused criminals while they are on trial, in order for the accused to be held as close to the courtroom as possible. In fact, many cities and towns have combined the functions into one building, so that a prisoner can simply be transferred from a cell in one part of the building to a courtroom in another part.

County and parish jails are usually associated with superior courts, which try cases up to and including murder. These are usually larger and more secure facilities designed to hold inmates whose sentences range up to one year.

What generally is referred to as a prison usually is a much larger and even more secure state or federal facility, often situated in a rural area in order to make it easier to contain possible escapes. There also are political reasons for putting prisons in rural areas, as few urbanites want to have a prison in their neighborhood. Prisons hold inmates with much longer sentences, including life sentences. And in states where the death penalty is used, often one prison will be designated for death row. This is effectively a prison within a prison, holding inmates who have been sentenced to death while their appeals are heard by higher courts.

Most states maintain their own prison systems. The federal government also maintains a network of prisons, including the supermaxes—super-maximum-security prisons where the most infamous of criminals are kept.

Even as the population swelled, the prison system continued to operate under the premise that incarceration was meant to punish. But there was a small group of reformers who thought that prisons should be dedicated to transforming prisoners and changing their lives.

In 1870, that prison reform movement gathered momentum with the founding of the National Prison Association, later called the American Correctional Association. Ohio governor Rutherford B. Hayes—who later was elected president of the United States— became head of the new association. Hayes called on prison leaders nationwide to institute reforms that would provide a more humane treatment of prisoners, offer them education and job training, and put an end to fixed sentences, which had been popular at the time. Such sentences stated an exact amount of time a prisoner must spend behind bars, without exception. In their stead came indeterminate sentences, in which judges sentenced criminals to a range of time behind bars. This allowed for some flexibility about when the criminals were released, based on factors such as how much they had reformed while in prison.

The meeting of the National Prison Association led to the establishment of a new correctional facility at Elmira, New York, which was directed by Zebulon Brockway. The Elmira Reformatory, which opened in 1876, housed younger prisoners, ages sixteen to thirty, who were serving their first prison terms. At Elmira, young offenders had the opportunity to receive an education and learn a vocational trade, such as knitting or shoemaking, so they could lead successful lives in the community. They also had the opportunity to receive a reduced sentence given as a reward for those who had demonstrated good behavior. Over the next four decades, several other states opened reformatories based on the Elmira system.

The Elmira Reformatory also led to the establishment of a separate court system for juvenile offenders. Exactly what age constituted a juvenile varied. Sometimes, the cutoff age was sixteen or seventeen; other times, it was eighteen or even nineteen. Regardless, beginning in Chicago in 1899, the new court system permitted judges to treat young offenders differently than adults. Youths were considered in the formative stages of development and not as responsible as adults for any crimes that they may have committed. Judges could put them on probation for minor crimes such as vandalism, simple assault, and petty theft. This meant the offender did not receive a prison sentence, but supervision by officers of the court. Meanwhile, the first juvenile prison opened at St. Charles, Illinois, in 1904. For the first time, juveniles found to have committed criminal offenses were placed in a separate institution—not in the same prison as adults.

At the same time, separate female prisons also were being constructed. The first was the Female Prison and Reformatory Institution for Girls and Women in Indianapolis, Indiana, in 1874. Another female prison opened in 1877 at Sherborn, Massachusetts. These prisons were significant because they allowed women to escape the sexual abuse many of them had been subjected to during the time they were locked up with men.

Parole, used extensively at Elmira, became a key element of the entire American prison system. This concept had been pioneered in Australia by Alexander Maconochie, head of that country's Norfolk Island prison. Maconochie had established a "mark system," enabling prisoners who acted responsibly to earn good marks, or good-time credits, that would shorten their sentences. The mark system acted as an incentive for prisoners to behave themselves while they were behind bars. Meanwhile, an Irish reformer named Sir Walter Crofton had instituted the "ticket-of-leave" system in Ireland. This system enabled prisoners to pass through a series of stages based on good behavior. Those stages began with solitary confinement and progressed to work in the outside community without supervision. Prisoners who performed well at each stage could be given a pardon, or ticket of leave, and win an early release from prison.

More Prisons, More Reform

Though reform was instituted in some prisons, most facilities continued to treat inmates harshly. As stated in *The American Prison*, overall prison life during the first quarter of the twentieth century continued to be characterized by "total control, punishment and hard labor." There were often few opportunities for prisoners to receive an education. Medical treatment for illness or injury was not adequate, and punishment for prisoners who disobeyed the rules was severe. Stephen Cox, author of the historical prison book, *The Big House*, wrote: "If you live in a nineteenth-century prison . . . you may be locked in a dark cell and kept there on rations of bread and water. You may be forced to take down your pants so you can be paddled like a schoolboy. You may be put in a cell with your wrists chained to the bars, and your nose pointed at a solid steel outer door . . . and be left there to stand for hours at a time." Regardless of how brutal such treatment may sound today, this still was acceptable to a majority of Americans at the time.

As prison populations continued to swell, more prisons were built. Between 1900 and 1925, thirty-one major prisons for adults were constructed nationwide. Meanwhile, the federal government also had begun constructing prisons to house criminals convicted of federal crimes, such as kidnapping and counterfeiting. Previously, federal prisoners had been held in state-run prisons, but that changed in 1887 after Congress prohibited federal prisoners from being used as workers for outside businesses. State prisons could no longer contract out their federal inmates and profits from their work, so they did not want to pay for their upkeep. Thus, a need arose for a system in which to house federal prisoners. In 1906, the first U.S. penitentiary opened at Fort Leavenworth, Kansas. Feder-

Puck, 1910

THE IN AND OUT OF OUR PENAL SYSTEM.
The law against them.   The world against them.

Cartoonist Al Young depicted the prison system in the United States in 1910 as something like the "Hotel California" — you could enter but could not really leave.

al prisons in Atlanta, Georgia, and on McNeil Island, Washington, followed. In 1930, the Federal Bureau of Prisons was established to oversee all eleven of the federal prisons in existence at the time.

Many of these prisons held people who had been convicted of violating prohibition laws, including the Eighteenth Amendment, which became effective in 1920. These laws prevented the manufacture, sale, and transportation of alcohol. However, prohibition was widely violated, especially by gangsters who realized that they could grow wealthy supplying alcohol to the millions of Americans who still wanted to drink. Bootlegging—the illegal manufacture and sale of alcohol—also led to violent conflicts between gangs of mobsters who tried to control the illegal alcohol industry. A similar situation exists today in the world of illegal drugs.

While the prison population was increasing, the jobs that prisoners were allowed to perform changed. In 1929, Congress passed the Hawes-Cooper Act, giving each state the right to prevent items from crossing its borders if those items were made in prisons located in other states. The act was passed because, thanks to free labor, convict-made goods were much cheaper than those goods produced by companies that used non-convict workers. Labor unions had huge problems with this competition. The Hawes-Cooper Act was strengthened in 1935 and again in 1940. As a result, prison work declined, leaving many prisoners with little to do while they were behind bars. During World War II, this law temporarily was relaxed so prisoners could make clothing and other items that were necessary to support American soldiers in combat. For example, shoes and boots were produced by prisoners at Fort Leavenworth, while aircraft engines were manufactured by prisoners at the Federal Reformatory in Chillicothe, Ohio.

Reforms: 1950s to 1970s

After World War II, a new reform movement began to again transform America's prisons. This coincided with advancements in the field of psychology that helped people to effectively deal with emotional problems. As the Joint Commission on Correctional Manpower and Training reported in 1970, "The offender was perceived as a person with social, intellectual, or emotional deficiencies who should be diagnosed carefully and his deficiencies clinically defined. Programs should be designed to correct these deficiencies to the point that would permit him to assume a productive, law-abiding place in the community." It was at this point that prisons began being referred to as "correctional institutions."

Prison health care soon began to improve. In addition, prisoners entering a correctional facility were diagnosed more carefully and separated from each other according to their diagnosed mental illnesses. New diagnostic centers opened at locations such as Menlo

Park, New Jersey, to test and evaluate entering prisoners. These facilities reflected advances in psychiatry and the understanding of mental illness that occurred during the twentieth century.

New prison facilities also were built to house prisoners who had committed different types of crimes. For example, maximum-security prisons—today known as supermax prisons—housed violent criminals, such as serial murderers and gang leaders. Prisoners there were kept locked in their cells, a condition called lockdown, for most of the day. Medium-security prisons housed inmates who had committed less-severe crimes. There, prisoners often slept in dormitories that were locked at night, ate in dining halls, and bathed in communal showers. Minimum-security prisons housed prisoners who had been convicted of so-called white-collar crimes, such as embezzling money, and nonviolent drug-related crimes. Since they were considered to pose little threat to society, these prisoners might have minimal supervision and might even be assigned to work on community projects.

Unfortunately, the increase in prison construction could not keep pace with the growing prisoner population and the problem of overcrowding. That was, in part, because of the growth of the illegal drug trade in the United States, as more people began using such substances, including cocaine. In 1971, President Richard Nixon declared a war on drugs, and drug-related arrests increased accordingly. By the mid-1970s, more than 200,000 people were incarcerated, nearly double the figure of just fifty years earlier.

Severe overcrowding was one of the factors that led to the brutal prison riot at the Attica Correctional Facility in New York in 1971. Prisoners there also complained about poor living conditions and racial prejudice by white guards toward black inmates. Overcrowding, along with poor sanitation and other factors, also played a key role in another severe riot, which broke out at the New Mexico State Penitentiary in 1980. That gruesome uprising resulted in the death of thirty-three prisoners.

The twenty-first century has seen the rise of the so-called "supermax" prison for violent offenders. Joseph Dole, an inmate in a supermax prison in Illinois, talks about his daily routine through the dime-sized holes which are the only light he gets through his cell door.

Some people argued that these events indicated that prison conditions still were in need of reform. Others argued that prisons still were not tough enough, and that prisoners needed to be placed under stronger restraints. One former prison aide told investigators after the New Mexico riot, "That prison was the most corrupt place on earth. I lived in fear of dying, because I knew that if I died while I worked in that place, I'd go straight to hell." The refining of America's prison system continued.

The Rights of Prisoners

Prison inmates have some, but not all, of the same constitutional rights as other American citizens. Inmates are not permitted to vote in elections, based on the theory that those people who are not able to follow the law certainly should not be allowed to help choose those who make it. The U.S. Supreme Court, in a series of decisions in the 1970s, defined the way that the U.S. Constitution protects the rights of American prisoners. In 1974, Justice Byron White wrote the majority opinion in the case of *Wolff* v. *McDonnell*, regarding a prisoner's right to retain or lose good-time credits that would shorten his or her sentence based on good behavior while behind bars. Charles Wolff Jr. and other prisoners in Nebraska claimed they had lost their good-time credits without due process of law—that is, the same procedures that other citizens living outside prison would have received. The Court determined that inmates are sometimes entitled to due process, depending on several factors, such as how serious the misconduct was.

In another case decided in 1974, *Procunier* v. *Martinez*, Justice William Powell delivered the majority opinion of the Supreme Court regarding mail censorship in prison. The Court ruled that prison administrators could not prevent a prisoner from receiving mail because that would violate the protection of free speech contained in the Bill of Rights of the Constitution.

Only mail that might undermine prison security or the rehabilitation of inmates can be censored. Determination of such is made by prison staff who open and examine the mail before distributing it.

In 1976, in *Estelle* v. *Gamble*, Justice Thurgood Marshall talked about medical care for prisoners. He wrote, "Deliberate indifference by prison personnel to a prisoner's serious illness or injury constitutes cruel and unusual punishment." This is a violation of the Eighth Amendment to the Constitution.

There have been many tough-on-crime laws that have taken away prisoners' rights as well, beginning in the 1980s, when a conservative Supreme Court was in place. In 1981, for example, in the case of *Rhodes* v. *Chapman*, the Supreme Court ruled in a majority decision written by Justice Powell that overcrowding is not unconstitutional. Justice Powell said, "The Constitution does not mandate comfortable prisons." In 1984, the Court ruled that the Fourth Amendment does not apply to prisoners. Therefore, they can be subject to searches and seizures of their property. In 1995, the Prison Litigation Reform Act placed limitations on how much prisoners could complain about conditions in their prisons, and made it harder for prisoners to file federal lawsuits. In 2009, the Supreme Court denied prisoners the right to use DNA testing in an attempt to prove their innocence after they had been found guilty. The Court said it was up to individual states to decide their own policies on the matter.

One of the biggest decisions by the Supreme Court came in 2010. It stated that, upon being arrested, once criminal suspects have been read their rights—known as Miranda rights—they must speak up to invoke those rights. Therefore, if they wish to remain silent or have an attorney present during their questioning, they must say so, otherwise whatever they tell police can be used against them later during any subsequent trials for their crime. Prior to the Supreme Court's 1966 decision in *Miranda* v. *Arizona*, police could question suspects as much as they wanted and pressure them into admitting to crimes. Miranda laws gave suspects more power during their initial questioning, but the 2010 ruling took back some of that power.

Other major recent Supreme Court decisions have abolished the death penalty for juvenile offenders, ruled that sex offenders can continue to be housed in general prisons, and barred life sentences without parole for juvenile offenders for crimes other than murder.

During the American colonial period, towns built jails to house prisoners who were awaiting corporal punishment—the infliction of painful measures, such as whipping or beating, on someone for disciplinary purposes—for their crimes. Today, corporal punishment may be considered inhumane by certain societies, but it was the norm at the time, being imposed even for minor crimes such as public intoxication.

But as corporal punishment disappeared by the end of the eighteenth century, local governments began constructing prisons to house criminals who were sentenced to spend time behind bars. During the nineteenth century, prisoners received training in various trades so they could lead successful lives in the community. Near the end of that century, a system of parole was introduced to reward prisoners who had demonstrated good behavior with release dates before their sentences were completed. Still, during the first quarter of the twentieth century, prison life continued to be perceived as a place where punishment was the first priority.

After World War II, prisons grew larger and larger. In time, prison became known, in slang, as "The Big House." Many Americans continued to believe that the primary task of prisons was to punish convicted criminals for their crimes. However, during the prosperous post-war years, sentiment was with those reformers who believed that prisons should be dedicated to transforming prisoners and changing their lives. The pendulum between reform and punishment continues to swing back and forth in the twenty-first century.

2 Prison Issues

TRISH BROCKMAN IS THE ASSISTANT WARDEN AT THE Nebraska Correctional Youth Facility in Omaha, Nebraska. The special institution is for young people who have been convicted of violent crimes. She came to the correctional facility following a lengthy career in adult corrections, and today she helps run an education program for the facility's youths. In 2008, Nebraska Correctional Youth Facility established a "Special Purpose School" accredited through the state's Department of Education, which offers young people a high school diploma after they pass courses taught by certified teachers at the correctional facility. Brockman said it has made a significant difference. This is "a sign of success for them," she said, "an accomplishment that they probably thought they'd never achieve. . . . They take pride in themselves; it's reflected everywhere, in school and on the prison yard." In 2009, the program graduated its first twelve students.

Brockman's work represents some of the positive efforts underway to rehabilitate those who live behind bars. Meanwhile, Senator Jim Webb, a Democrat from Virginia, launched an investigation into the negative aspects of America's prisons. Webb said the U.S. prison system is currently incarcerating people who are mentally ill as well as those with drug problems—two groups of people he does not believe belong behind bars. In addition, Webb said, prisoners must deal with inhumane conditions, and they are often subjected to rape and other forms of violence. Furthermore, those who leave prison are frequently more violent and less suited for meaningful work than they were when they entered. Finally, Webb pointed out that the United States has the highest rate of incarceration of any nation in the world. "We have 5 percent of the world's population," Webb said, "and 25 percent of the people in prison. Either we're the most evil people on earth, or we're doing something wrong." In 2009, Webb introduced legislation that would establish a commission to investigate the current criminal justice system in America and to propose reforms. Webb's bill has support from both Democrats and Republicans alike.

As indicated by Assistant Warden Brockman's and Senator Webb's involvement, there are issues currently being raised about U.S. prisons by people who think they need to be changed. Some of these issues are listed below.

- Why were prisons established in the United States and what are they designed to accomplish?
- Why has the prison population increased so drastically over the past several decades, and does this increase make sense?
- What are the current conditions inside America's prisons and do they need to be improved?
- What are the conditions for undocumented immigrants inside America's prisons?
- How do we handle juvenile offenders, such as those at the Nebraska Correctional Youth Facility, and does our treatment of them promote rehabilitation?
- How well does the parole system work?
- What, if anything, can be done to make prisons more effective in serving the inmate population and the rest of American society?

Of course, there are those who believe prisons are fine the way they are, serving society well by focusing on punishing criminals. Noted criminologist Charles H. Logan, author of *Private Prisons: Cons and Pros*, is among them. He believes: "Prisons should not try to be 'correctional institutions.' . . . The message of a prison should be simple: 'Felonies are wrong and controllable acts, and those who commit them will be punished.' Institutions aiming for 'rehabilitation' more often transmit this muddled message: 'Felonies are the result of social and personal deficiencies . . . and society has a responsibility to correct these deficiencies.' . . . Such a message may excuse, and even encourage, crime; at the very least, it weakens the vital punishment messages of imprisonment."

The Exploding Prison Population

Over the past hundred years or so, the number of prisoners in correctional facilities has grown steadily. The upward trend began during the 1920s, as a result of rising unemployment and violations of prohibition laws. In 1918, for example, there were approximately eighty-two people in prison per 100,000 in population. By 1940, that number had risen to 132 for every 100,000 people. And the numbers continued to grow. By the first decade of the twenty-first century, more than 700 people were in prison for every 100,000, for a total of 2.3 million people behind bars in 2008. By way of comparison, there are 40 percent more people jailed in the United States than there are in Russia, the country with the next-highest number of prisoners. More than 700,000 American prisoners are in local jails—for minor offenses like traffic violations, or awaiting trial or sentencing for more serious offenses. The rest of the inmates, nearly 1.6 million, are in state and federal prisons.

The reasons for these large numbers vary. One is the large number of people imprisoned for drug offenses. In addition, many states as well as the federal government have greatly reduced the possibility of parole and passed mandatory sentencing

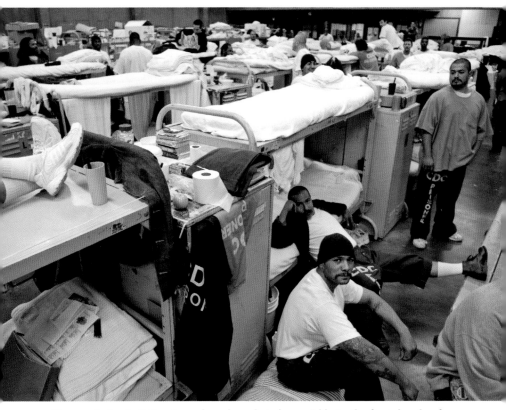

The population in U.S. prisons has skyrocketed so quickly in the first decade of the twenty-first century that there isn't enough room to hold all the prisoners. Inmates in Folsom Prison in California are crammed into gymnasiums converted into dormitories to hold the overflow.

laws—regulations that require those convicted of drug offenses and other crimes to serve a fixed sentence without parole. Finally, many states have passed so-called three strikes laws that imprison for life those convicted of a third offense.

A large percentage of these prisoners are African American. One of every eleven African Americans is currently under the control of the prison system, compared to only one of thirty-one Americans overall. Women are the fastest growing population behind bars.

The increased effort to imprison offenders has been driven by a belief that incarceration will reduce the amount of crime and make the general population safer. In fact, states have increased their spending on new prisons by more than 300 percent in the last twenty years. While crime has declined during that period, it is a long way from being eliminated in the United States.

Conditions Inside Prisons

The rise in prison population has led to worsening conditions—such as more disease and more violence—inside prisons. The problem is especially bad in California, which has the second-largest prison population in the United States. The state's inmates are confined in correctional facilities that were built to handle only half the current number of prisoners, which stands at around 170,000. Another cause of overcrowding is the fact that many prisons are housing more and more undocumented immigrants. In 2009, the California legislature passed a new law aimed at cutting the prison population by shortening sentences and making parole more easily available to people convicted of nonviolent crimes. These measures are designed to save the state $1 billion in its corrections budget, which stood at roughly $10 billion per year.

Although the California bill was passed into law, not everyone was in favor of reducing prison time. Law enforcement groups objected to the measure, and ran advertisements to that effect. One such ad was directed at then governor Arnold Schwarzenegger. It read: "For the past few years, you've been quietly dumping more and more parolees on the street, with less and less supervision and no business being free. Now 17-year-old Lily Burk is dead." Burk had been found murdered in the summer of 2009 in Los Angeles. A state parolee was arrested on suspicion of the killing and eventually pleaded guilty to the murder.

Juvenile Justice

Another hotly debated issue of today is the American corrections system's treatment of juvenile offenders. Each of the fifty states has

A makeshift memorial for Lily Burk, who was abducted while running an errand for her mother. She was killed within hours by a fifty-year-old transient with a long criminal record.

established a special court system to handle juvenile offenders under the age of eighteen. However, every state allows a juvenile accused of a violent crime to be tried as an adult in certain instances, such as if they are accused of murder. Those who are convicted under those circumstances receive adult sentences that may put them in prison for many years, even for life, though in 2010 the U.S. Supreme Court barred life sentences for juveniles unless they had committed murder.

Like adults, juveniles sent to youth prisons, or separate facilities for juveniles, also have been subjected to harsh treatment by prison officials, according to at least one study conducted in New York. In addition, many states have cut their budgets for mental health care during the recent recession. As a result, juvenile offenders with mental illness are increasingly being sent to juvenile prisons instead of being treated by community mental health facilities. And such prisons have been criticized for not having enough therapists on hand.

The U.S. Parole System

Since the end of the nineteenth century, prisons have used parole as a way of rewarding inmates for good behavior. While tougher sentencing laws have reduced the number of parolees, convicts on parole currently number more than 800,000. In California in 2009, for example, corrections officials planned to release more prisoners into the parole system to reduce overcrowding in prisons. Many previously had been on parole and then returned to prison after violating their parole by committing nonviolent offenses, such as failing a drug test.

Nevertheless, the parole system itself is overburdened. Many parole officers already have large caseloads, which reduces the amount of attention that they can give to each parolee. Community services also are frequently inadequate in helping parolees deal with substance abuse problems, find jobs, or locate a place to live. However, efforts are underway in many states through community agencies, churches, and other groups to help inmates after they leave prison and reenter the community. This is all aimed at reducing the rate at which parolees return to prison—called recidivism—which is about 67 percent of all those who were released from state prisons. The reasons for such high rates vary, but in general, proponents of rehabilitation believe it is due to prisoners not receiving enough education and treatment while they are incarcerated.

Many people in positions of authority believe that taking such a stance, which labels the criminal victim and blames the state's lack of in-prison aid for the high recidivism rate, is not the correct philosophy. Dan Lungren, the former attorney general of California and now a Republican member of Congress from that state, believes focusing too much on the rights of criminals undermines the entire purpose of the criminal justice system, which is to protect innocent people from crime. In 1996, Lungren wrote, "A criminal justice system that contorts itself to the extreme in a purported effort 'to protect the accused,' with the result that the innocent victim is denied justice (which includes retribution), is a system which has lost its sight and soul and forfeited its right to be called 'just' or justice. . . . I urge you not to forget the true victims of crime: those who have been violently assaulted by others, and the families of victims."

3 Current Prison Conditions

DURING THE EARLY 1980S, LIAM Q. SERVED ABOARD an aircraft carrier in the United States Navy. While he was on shore leave in Norfolk, Virginia, he began an affair with a married woman. In 1983, at age nineteen, he was convicted of murdering the woman's husband and given a life sentence in prison. At the time, a life sentence meant that, with good behavior and the ability to show a parole board he had changed, Liam might only serve eighteen or nineteen years in prison. Unlike the husband he murdered, Liam had the possibility of finally returning to society.

About ten years later, that possibility of one day leaving prison vanished for a majority of lifers—those serving life sentences—when forty states, including Virginia, passed "truth-in-sentencing" laws, also known as determinate sentences. With regard to life sentences, the new laws meant that anyone given a life sentence would be expected to serve as much as 85 percent of it before being considered for parole. This was part of a nationwide trend to get tough with criminals brought about when advocacy groups and the public at large began to demand an ability to know exactly how long convicted criminals would be behind bars. As an extra incentive to enact these new laws, Congress passed the Violent Crime Control and Law Enforcement Act in 1994. Under this legislation, states were offered additional funds to construct new prisons if they adopted truth-in-sentencing laws.

There is little dispute that truth-in-sentencing laws and an increased number of prisoners serving life sentences are among the reasons that the prison population has soared over the past fifteen years. California, with its approximately 170,000 inmates, currently has 34,164 people serving life sentences. Nationwide, the number of prisoners serving life sentences has jumped from about 34,000 in 1984 to 140,610 in 2008, out of a total prison population of 2.3 million.

After many legal rulings against it, California was ordered by a panel of federal judges to reduce the number of prisoners in its overcrowded facilities and provide sufficient medical care for inmates. One specific example of California's overcrowding can be found at Folsom State Prison in the city of Folsom. Folsom currently holds 3,540 men in a facility designed for 2,085, and there are fifteen to twenty documented assaults among prisoners each week. In reaction to the federal ruling, Governor Schwarzenegger promised to reduce the prison population by granting parole to prisoners convicted of nonviolent crimes. The federal prison system does not offer parole to those serving life sentences. Neither do Illinois, Iowa, Louisiana, Maine, Pennsylvania, or South Dakota. California does offer parole to lifers; however, it has a reputation of rarely granting that parole.

This increase in life sentences without parole also has meant that an increasing number of prisoners are middle aged or elderly. As reported in 2009 by the Sentencing Project—a nonprofit group that monitors prison conditions—the number of prisoners over the age of fifty has doubled since the 1990s. Specific numbers are difficult to come by because there is no standard definition set for what constitutes an "older" prisoner. Some studies and states use the age of fifty, others use fifty-five. Society in general uses the age of sixty-five. By any definition, and because people tend to need more medical care as they age, these older prisoners cost the taxpayers more to take care of. The costs vary from state to state. In California, the cost for prisoners over fifty-five is between $98,000 and $138,000 per year.

Another factor that has led to an increase in the prison population is mandatory minimum sentencing laws that began to be approved by state legislatures in the 1970s during President Nixon's war on drugs. The new laws meant that judges no longer had wide discretion in passing sentences on convicted criminals. Under the mandatory sentencing laws, they were required to hand down sentences that followed the guidelines in the laws. For example, these laws require that anyone convicted of possession of five grams of crack cocaine will receive a minimum sentence of 5 years in prison. To illustrate, 5 grams of crack cocaine, about the equivalent of less than two sugar packets commonly found in restaurants, is good for approximately twenty-five doses, depending on the user.

President Richard M. Nixon's war on drugs led to a surge in prison populations that shows few, if any, signs of slowing down.

As a result of mandatory sentencing laws and the war on drugs, the number of drug offenders arrested annually almost quadrupled from 1970—to about 2 million during the first decade of the twenty-first century. Thanks to the relative ease of catching small-time users, as well as the sheer numbers of such individuals, the vast majority of the people serving sentences were not dealers or so-called drug kingpins—gang leaders—but people caught using illegal drugs.

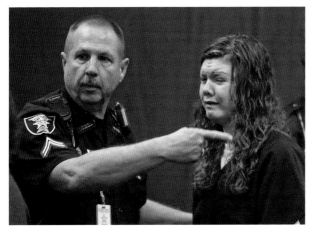

Nineteen-year-old Hope Sykes is taken away in tears after being sentenced to the mandatory minimum sentence in Florida of fifteen years in prison on one charge of drug trafficking.

The Sentencing Project has reported that a large proportion of the people behind bars for drug offenses are African Americans. While they are only 13 percent of the population, they comprise 35 percent of those arrested for drug abuses. The National Survey on Drug Use and Health, a study sponsored by the U.S. Department of Health and Human Services, reports that the reason for this is that African Americans are more likely to live in urban areas and buy drugs on the street, where they can more easily be picked up by police.

In 2009, Alton Maddox, a black rights activist and prominent former lawyer whose law license was suspended in 1990, wrote an opinion piece in the *New York Amsterdam News*, a well-known New York newspaper catering to blacks. He wrote that more black men are locked behind bars in prison than are enrolled in college. Maddox, who is black, pointed out that the average annual cost of keeping an inmate in prison—$29,000—is higher than the average annual cost of a college education. Maddox's implication was that the black population is getting short shrift and America's priorities are out of whack with regard to his race, especially when it comes to the judicial system.

Prison populations also have increased due to the three strikes laws that have been passed by some states. In Washington State, for example, a third felony conviction—regardless of what crime was committed—leads to a life sentence behind bars. Those who believe such mandates are too strict commonly point to stories of people who have been sentenced to life in prison on the basis of rather minor crimes. People such as Mary Thompson, for example, who was convicted of stealing tracksuits from a store in 1982 to support her drug addiction. Yet because it was her third felony conviction, she received a life sentence and will have no chance of parole until 2020.

Despite its perceived flaws, many policymakers believe strongly that the three strikes law is the way to operate. R. David LaCourse Jr. is among them. As executive director of Washington Citizens for Justice, LaCourse played an integral role in drafting Washington's three strikes law, which became the first such law in the United States when it was enacted in 1993. Four years after the law was on the books, LaCourse wrote: "Many police officers, corrections officers and others, both inside and outside the criminal justice system, have noted that criminals fear Three Strikes. These people have also found that some criminals have modified their behavior. For once, felons are worried about the criminal justice system and that has proven to be a deterrent factor. . . . Washington's Three Strikes law has worked as intended. The law is incarcerating violent, career criminals who are unlikely to change their behavior."

Above all, it is women who comprise the fastest growing segment of people in prisons. Between 1977 and 2004, the number of women behind bars increased by 757 percent to almost 100,000. Many of these women were convicted of drug offenses. Wrote one author on the subject, "[J]udges have little discretion to consider the level or circumstances of women's involvement in an underlying drug offense, even though women very rarely play a central role in the drug trade. Women of color have been disproportionately affected. In 2005, black women were more than three times as likely as white women to be incarcerated, and Latina women were 60 percent more likely."

In 2002, a group called Families to Amend California's Three Strikes led a protest against the three-strikes law.

Exploding Population and Poor Conditions

Between 2007 and 2008, the national prison population reached about 1.6 million. The states of California, Texas, Florida, and New York have the largest numbers of inmates. And five states, Connecticut, Delaware, Michigan, Oregon, and Vermont, increased the funds spent on prisons by more than 100 percent in the two decades between 1987 and 2007. As a result, these states found themselves spending more on prisons than on higher education. Some people, such as Maddox, see this as a problem.

Housing prison populations also has become very expensive. States spent about $18.65 billion on prisons in 2008, or around 90 percent of all money spent on corrections. Only about $2.5 billion was spent on probation or parole. The severe economic recession that began in 2008 forced states to look carefully at the amount of money spent on correctional systems to try to cut costs. California passed legislation reducing its prison population by 11,000 in order to save about $220 million annually, and also to conform to federal rulings requiring them to do so. But such cuts would only slightly ease the burden on the state's overcrowded prisons, which held twice as many prisoners as they were built to contain. One obvious answer would be to build more prisons, but doing so costs money that cash-strapped states do not have.

By no means is prison overcrowding a new issue. Overcrowding has been growing worse for more than three decades. By 1982, forty-two states had been ordered by the federal courts to improve prison conditions because of overcrowding, poor levels of health care, deteriorating housing, and other problems. Although states added more prisons, the problems frequently were not solved, because the prison population also increased.

In 1975, the prison population in the United States stood at roughly 100 per 100,000. By 2008, that number had skyrocketed to more than 700 per 100,000. As a result, conditions have continued to deteriorate inside many prison facilities. The *Economist* magazine reported that one-fifth of all U.S. prisoners stated that they were sexually abused by other inmates or prison guards and that there are four times as many mentally ill people in prison as there are in mental hospitals.

One of the least attractive side effects of incarceration can be found in America's households, where families are broken apart and incomes decline when a family member, typically the male breadwinner, is in prison. Today, there are approximately 1.7 million children with a parent in prison. In 2009, the *Economist* re-

Riot at California Prison

In August 2009, inmates at the California Institution for Men in Chino—just east of Los Angeles—rioted against the prison authorities. The prison contains seven units, with about 200 inmates in each unit. Approximately 250 inmates were injured before prison guards brought the riot under control.

Some two years earlier, at least one national expert had warned a special federal panel of judges that overcrowding at Chino had led to a situation where "a serious disturbance [was] waiting to happen. If the prisoners wanted to take over the dorm they could do so in a second and no one would know."

Facilities that were built to house three thousand inmates contained almost twice that number. Tensions erupted among some of the prisoners, leading to a fight, which grew worse because of overcrowding, and then led to the riot. Some people believe overcrowding was to blame for the altercations, while others were not so sure. California's prisons spokesperson said, "I kind of chuckle when I hear people say, 'Well, overcrowding caused this.' No, misbehaving caused it and they didn't get into prison for behaving in the first place."

ported that such children are six times more likely than their peers to end up in prison.

The reasons for incarcerations—as *Corrections Today*, the official publication of the American Correctional Association, stated—range "from society's desire for retribution to its belief in rehabilitation. . . . In either case, the ultimate purpose is to improve public safety." If prisoners believe they will be punished, they may be less likely to commit future crimes. If they are reformed as a result of prison stays, they may turn away from crime to pursue other livelihoods.

One study published in 2006 in the journal *Criminology & Public Policy* investigated whether the increase in incarceration actually improves safety—that is, reduces crime. Looking at prison and crime statistics from 1972 through 2000, the study found that the effect of prison growth on crime diminishes as the scale of imprisonment increases. The scale tips away from reducing crime once the rate of imprisonment reaches about 325 prisoners per 100,000. Beyond that, increasing the rate of incarceration does not impact crime figures. One of the reasons for this is that new inmates admitted in the past when prison populations were small tended to be primarily violent and property offenders. Removing such people from society obviously would have an impact on crime in communities. But recently, prisoners have tended to be mainly drug offenders. Removing them from society has had a smaller effect on crime rates in communities, the study showed.

Due to the economic recession that began in 2008, the quality of life behind bars has deteriorated. Kenneth Hartman, author of *Mother California: A Story of Redemption Behind Bars*, was sentenced to life without parole for murder in 1980. In his book, he wrote that the quantity and quality of prison food—which is chock-full of potatoes and meat substitutes—has markedly decreased, and added that even before the recession, prisoners in the California system "lost most of the positive programs, like conjugal [spousal] visits and college education that we had had since the '70s." He added that, during the summer, the air-conditioning broke in the visiting room and 150 people had to put up with heat that regularly hits 100 degrees °F (38 °C).

Proponents of punishment would counter Hartman's story with the point that life behind bars is not supposed to be filled with all the conveniences people enjoy outside prison. After all, inmates are there because they committed crimes, thereby forfeiting their right to live what they previously would have defined as a "normal" life. Many people believe the goal is to make prisons places people want to avoid at all costs. Former Republican congressman Richard "Dick" Zimmer of New Jersey is one of them. He said, "Some criminals have come to view jail as an almost acceptable lifestyle because amenities are better for them on the inside than on the outside. When you break the law of the land, you should pay the price for your crime, not be rewarded with a vacation watching premium cable on your personal television."

Prison Privatization

The recession has led states to look for alternative ways to deal with current prison conditions and the shortage of funds available to improve them. Thus, the age-old debate of privatizing correctional facilities has come back to the forefront. Arizona is a prime example of this. The state spends about $4.7 million annually on its prison system. The ten prisons in the state hold an estimated 40,000 inmates. In 2009, Arizona legislators began to consider putting the prison system into private hands to save public expenditures. The private operators would then be paid by the state for each prisoner they housed behind bars.

However, some legislators are skeptical about the impact of privatizing prisons. In the past, when efforts at privatization were made, states did not realize large savings. In addition, some prison officials are worried that private facilities cannot deal with violent

Overcrowding
in Jails

Prisons are not the only correctional institutions suffering from overcrowding. Local jails run by county and city governments are suffering, too. In 2009, approximately 750,000 inmates were being kept behind bars in local jails because they could not afford to pay bail, the money that those who are arrested must pay to the court in exchange for the ability to remain free until trial. An in-depth report done in 2010 by National Public Radio stated that the cost of keeping these people behind bars is $9 billion annually. To put a human face on the issue, the report cited the case of Leslie Chew, who was arrested in December 2008 for stealing blankets he said he wanted to use to keep himself warm while he slept in the back of his car in Lubbock, Texas. Chew was expected to pay $3,500 bail, but did not have the money, so he spent more than six months in jail waiting for his trial. It cost more than $7,000 to clothe, house, and feed him during that time. The purpose of the report was to show that often more serious criminals with access to enough money to post bail can remain free until their trial dates, while poor people who may only have committed petty crimes clog the already overcrowded jails.

criminals. James Austin, who helped lead a study by the Department of Justice, explained that private companies have experience with minimum- and medium-security prisons but not with maximum-security facilities.

As of 2010, approximately 100,000 inmates were in prisons under private operation. Approximately 50 percent of all states as well as the federal government rely to some degree on privately run prisons. There were more than 200 of these facilities. In 2007, at a meeting sponsored by the National Institute of Justice, attendees considered studies of private prisons and their effectiveness. These studies differed on the costs of a privately owned facility—one showing that the facility was almost 15 percent cheaper to operate than prisons that were publicly run, while the other showed only a 2 percent cost savings. The reason for the difference was that the privately run prison had more prisoners each year than the publicly run facility. Another study took this into account in comparing costs and calculated that economies of scale made the difference in average cost per prisoner. If the difference in the number of prisoners annually had been eliminated, cost differences only would have been about 2 percent.

However, a study of a privately run federal prison in California showed there was an estimated 6 to 10 percent cost savings versus a publicly run institution. In addition, studies compiled by the same national institute showed that the number of assaults among prisoners in the privately run prison was lower than the average number of assaults in the publicly run prison, although the researchers were quick to point out that the type of criminals in each prison would need to be taken into account before the evidence could be called conclusive. Yet the study also showed that medical care was more readily available and sought by more prisoners at the privately run facility. Correctional staffs were equally well-trained at private and public facilities.

Orange County, California, deputies worked on Christmas Day at the Intake and Release Center to move prisoners out of their holding cells.

4 Prison Health Care and Education

WHEN A CRIMINAL IS SENTENCED TO PRISON, HE or she passes through a prison intake system. Since about 45,000 males are admitted to prison each month, compared to about 5,500 females, there are more processing centers for men than women. And, in a majority of instances, there are different facilities for each sex, although a few states do have facilities that process both males and females. In Texas, which has the largest prison population in the United States, there are twenty-four intake facilities. That is almost twice the number of any other state.

As part of the process—which takes less than two weeks in some states and more than half a year in Hawaii—the prisoners are fingerprinted and photographed, and their personal items are noted and taken by the staff and then put in the prisoners' personal files. A team of experts at an intake facility may recommend the type of confinement, such as minimum or maximum security, where the inmate should serve his or her sentence. This classification system is based on a set of standards that score each inmate the same way. In addition, qualified medical professionals assess the mental and physical health of each inmate. This assessment includes a physical examination and an evaluation for addiction problems such as alcohol or drug abuse. This information helps determine any special health care or mental health programs that a prisoner may require while serving time in a correctional institution.

In Colorado, for example, the intake process takes fourteen days. During the first three days, a prisoner is given tests to determine his or her physical health, educational background and potential for learning, and substance abuse problems. In addition, the prison's gang coordinator looks for any evidence that the prisoner may be part of a gang—a group that can be violent and may cause other types of problems in correctional facilities. Over the next few days, office staff writes up a summary on the prisoner, who is then transferred to a prison to serve out his or her time. That facility— for example, maximum, medium, or minimum security—should reflect the risk that the prisoner may pose to society because of his or her crime, and provide programs that fulfill the prisoner's needs for health care, vocational training, and education.

Health Care in Prisons

Broderick Crawford cracked one of his teeth in California's Corcoran State Prison, where he was serving a sentence for attempted murder. Instead of going to the prison dentist, he decided to wait two years until he was released from prison to get dental care. He did not have any confidence in the prison dentist. "To put it bluntly," said California state senator Jackie Speier, "the health care system at CDC (California Department of Corrections) is sick. Twenty percent of the physicians that work at CDC have either a bad mark on their record or a series of malpractice lawsuits [from patients accusing them of poor medical care]—a figure that is four to five times higher than the general population of physicians in California."

However, doctors who work in the California correctional system disagree. They emphasize that the care they provide is just as good as the care patients receive in the communities from which the prisoners came. The prison doctors also point out that they face some handicaps that medical practitioners outside bars do not have to deal with, such as often having to use outdated and inadequate equipment. Despite this, many prisoners believe the medical care they receive is more than adequate. Clyde Hoffman, a prisoner in California, is one of them. In 2004, while receiving treatment for lung cancer, he said, "Everybody that works up here is excellent—this is far beyond my hopes and dreams that there'd be a place like this in prison." And even if prison dental and medical care is subpar compared to non-prison care, one thing is certain: it still is better than having no care.

In 2006, the California prison health care system was ordered by federal judge Thelton Henderson to reform its operations. Henderson based his decision on years of personal observations and anecdotes he had heard from others. "I would tell politicians all the time," Henderson said, "Don't you understand there are people dying in prison every day because of diseases like asthma that are easily treatable? And they'd say that they understood but they had to be careful, because they couldn't be seen 'to hug a thug.'" Since that time, more than sixty doctors have been fired for incompetence, new physicians have been hired, and corrections officers are making a much greater effort to ensure that inmates get to their medical appointments (the inmates' fear of being disciplined for not going being a big incentive). Prior to the reforms, one staff member estimated that 50 percent of patients did not make it to medical appointments because guards did not get them there on time.

Health Care for a Unique Population

The situation in California reflects a debate over prison health care that relates not only to the quality of care but also to its availability. Results of a nationwide survey released in 2009 titled *The Health and Health Care of U.S. Prisoners* provided a snapshot of health care in state and federal correctional institutions as well as in jails. The survey focused on a variety of health care issues, such as prisoners' access to medical examinations, prescription medicines, and emergency care for wounds or broken bones. It also focused on people with chronic illnesses.

Many people who are sent to correctional institutions suffer from chronic illnesses, such as heart ailments, diabetes, and asthma. One of the reasons is that they tend to be members of lower income groups that have not been able to afford medical care in the past. For many of the same reasons, prisoners also are more likely to have substance abuse issues and a need to be treated for them.

The survey further revealed that about 14 to 20 percent of state and federal prison inmates who were chronically ill had not received any medical exams in prison, and a large percentage of local jail inmates had not been examined. Among those with mental health problems who had been taking medication, only about 69 percent of state and federal inmates continued to receive their prescriptions.

Well-known political reporter Michael Crowley, who also is a columnist for *Reader's Digest*, believes prisoners receive too much health care treatment, particularly when compared to the tens of millions of Americans who have no health insurance coverage whatsoever. In 2004, Crowley wrote: "Around the country, hardened criminals of every stripe receive top-notch care that many average families don't get, including expensive dental surgery. In Oregon, which has recently cut public health benefits, the state is spending about $120,000 per year on dialysis treatments for a convicted murderer on death row. In other words, it's shelling out big bucks to keep him alive until it's time to kill him. . . . [W]hy are his costly treatments guaranteed and fully covered when plenty of law-abiding people can't afford the care they need? . . . [S]urely criminals shouldn't be rewarded with better coverage than law-abiding people, who deal with ever-stricter managed-care plans. . . . Premium health care shouldn't be the reward for robbing a bank." It should be noted that, because the person is incarcerated and incapable of taking care of his or her own health needs, the state is responsible for doing so.

As it is in society at large, the cost of health care is the fastest-growing category of prison operations. In addition to the overall increase in health care costs in the United States, another reason the cost of prison health care is rising is that more and more elderly prisoners are serving life sentences, thus increasing the number of patients suffering from diseases such as HIV. The report explained that because of skyrocketing costs, many prison systems are struggling to provide adequate health care to the rising number of inmates living in correctional institutions. In 2009, the average annual health care cost per prisoner over the age of fifty was about $70,000. Younger prisoners cost the prison system about one-third this amount.

The challenge for prison health care systems may be greater than that faced by medical care in the community outside prison walls. As Gary Maynard, president of the American Correctional Association, wrote in *Corrections Today*, "In many cases, correctional health care workers are treating inmates affected by life on the streets or in dangerous communities. They are treating intravenous drug users and the malnourished, both the underfed and those whose intake has little nutritional value. Many inmates never received childhood immunizations (for diseases like polio) and few have regular medical examinations."

That fact does not bother many Americans, including columnist Crowley, who believes, "The only class of people with a constitutional right to health care in the United States are prison inmates. For the roughly one in seven Americans living without coverage, their best hope of seeing a doctor for free might be getting thrown behind bars."

Some prisons are doing their best to deal with health care problems of inmates in their institutions. "Correctional health care is on the forefront of the battle against sexually transmitted diseases, including HIV/AIDS," wrote Maynard. "The scope of mental health disorders for which treatment is available in institutions surpasses that available to indigents in the community, and prisons constitute the largest source of residential mental health treatment available in the country."

Indeed, about one-half of all federal and state prison inmates had mental health problems at the time that they entered correctional institutions, one survey reported. Nevertheless, mental health care is limited, writes Chris Koyanagi, policy director at the Bazelon Center for Mental Health Law, a nonprofit group that works on behalf of those with mental illness. He said, "There's so much opportunity for prevention. But it seems we always want to wait, especially in mental health, until there's an emergency before we intervene." The Department of Justice reported that about 25 percent of those inmates with mental illness are repeat offenders. Koyanagi pointed out that many such inmates have grown up without proper care, committed crimes, and returned to prison again and again. "You have all of these issues and then you get arrested. It's just one long trajectory of misery."

The number of mentally ill prisoners has increased dramatically over the past half century. There are numerous reasons for this, including cuts that have taken place in the number of community services offered to the mentally ill and cuts that have been made in the number of mental institutions available, thanks to new medicines that have made diseases such as schizophrenia more manageable. The number of mentally ill in institutions has shrunk from 339 per 100,000 in 1955 to 29 per 100,000 in 1998. Many of those people who would have been in mental institutions fifty years ago are now in prisons instead.

Sometimes individuals with mental health and substance abuse problems are treated in the community and released, only to commit crimes and receive jail sentences. A study of women in this situation revealed that many were given medication in jail or at a mental health facility and released, with instructions to continue getting medical care in the community. However, these women, many of whom used crack cocaine, often did not continue treatment and were rearrested. Then they were given medication again. This happens both because it often is difficult to obtain medical

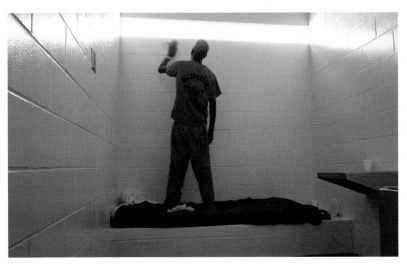

The number of mentally ill prisoners has shot up dramatically over the last fifty years. Here, a mentally ill prisoner cleans his cell wall, though it is not dirty, while under psychiatric observation.

care in the community at large and because those with mental health problems—once left to their own devices—often do not seek help or follow up on suggested treatment plans.

After repeatedly seeing the same women run through its system, the Sheriff's Office in Davidson County, Tennessee—the law-enforcement authority that oversees the county jail—tried a different approach. When asked why they used crack cocaine, many of the women blamed mental illness. Then, when they were locked up, those same women said they substituted for the crack they had used while on the street the legal medication they received from doctors for their illness. Under the new approach, once in jail, such prisoners were forced to stop using crack and taken off any prescribed medications they were taking for various illnesses. Then they were watched closely and given medication only if severe problems occurred. However, "many of the women learned . . . that they can cope well without legal or illegal drugs." Mental illness was not the key problem for this particular group of women; substance abuse had been the problem.

In addition to coping with mental illness and substance abuse, correctional institutions also must deal with the problem of HIV/AIDS. The number of AIDS cases in prison is estimated to be more than twice the rate in the community at large. Almost 50 percent of inmates with AIDS reside in prisons located in three states—Florida, New York, and Texas— and many of these inmates are African American and Hispanic. As the *American Journal of Public Health* reported in 2008, "[all types of] sexual intercourse occurs in prisons, even when prohibited." Yet only the Vermont and Mississippi state prison systems allow prisoners to have condoms that might enable them to prevent AIDS. The journal explained that there are several reasons for this approach. Prison officials believe that making HIV prevention information, as well as condoms, available might be "directly contradicting policies that prohibit . . . sex, condom use, and injection drug use in prisons." In addition, prison systems are dealing with tight budgets and "'nonessential programming' such as HIV prevention programs are the first to be eliminated."

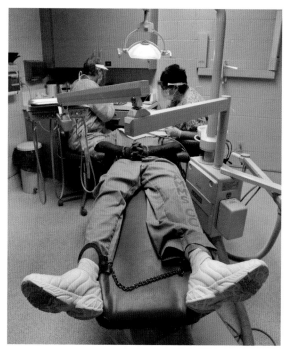

Prisons are responsible for the health of their prisoners, including their dental health, but some prisoners are so dangerous they are treated in shackles.

Elderly
Prisoners

George Sanges, seventy-three years old and afflicted with cerebral palsy, was given a fifteen-year prison sentence after being convicted of assaulting his wife. Sanges is counted among those inmates fifty-five and older—a prison population that has increased by more than 80 percent in the past decade, as reported by the Bureau of Justice. "With the elderly population, we're beginning to run something comparable to nursing homes," said Sharon Lewis, medical director for the Georgia Department of Corrections. "This is one of the unhealthiest populations found anywhere."

Lucille Keppen, at age ninety-two in 2006, was Minnesota's oldest inmate. She was eighty-eight when she shot and wounded her adopted son. She earned her GED in prison, and was released in 2007.

Six states have prisons set aside for older inmates, sometimes defined as those above age fifty and other times defined as those fifty-five or older. Ohio, for example, established the Hocking Correctional Facility for these inmates. Because of health care and nursing needs, the daily cost for an older prisoner is $81, which is $12 more than the daily cost for other inmates. At the Oakwood Correctional Facility in Ohio, there also is a special unit for prisoners over the age of fifty that treats those with physical illnesses and those suffering from dementia-related problems. Thirteen states have similar special units. Experts point out that prisons need health care workers with special training to deal with elderly prisoners. They must be able to spot those who are beginning to suffer from senility or depression or those who might be considering suicide. These problems are more common among older prisoners than the rest of the inmate population.

Older patients also do better in less-crowded prisons, with daily exercise programs and chances to interact with other prisoners and with members of their own families. But with budget cuts occurring in most states because of the economic recession, it's unlikely that facilities that cater exclusively to the needs of older inmates will be built.

While many in American society feel sympathy upon hearing about the rough life sick and elderly prisoners often have to deal with, others do not care at all. Foremost among them are the families of the victims. "Why should they be in a nursing home where their family gets to come and comfort them and say good-bye to them at their death bed? I can't say goodbye to my loved one," Shawn Chambers-Galis of Pennsylvania told the *Philadelphia Daily News* in 2006, in response to a story the newspaper was doing on a bill that would grant "compassionate release" to terminally ill inmates. "[An early release is] not what my justice system assured me would happen. I will agree with this the day they show me my brother's appeal process to get out of his grave." Chambers-Galis's brother and another man were shot and killed by an acquaintance in Alaska.

Prison Education

Many prison inmates lack even the high school education that might have enabled them to find steady employment before being incarcerated. Prior to 1965, few prisons provided any educational opportunities for prisoners. The riot at Attica Prison in 1971, followed by prison reform, changed that situation. Correctional facilities offered prisoners courses that enabled them to obtain high school equivalency diplomas. Meanwhile, Congress had also enacted a new law that offered prisoners financial aid if they took college courses. As stated by author Marlene Martin, national director of the Campaign to End the Death Penalty, "it was enough to sustain college education programs in 90 percent of states."

Then, in 1994, Congress passed new legislation, the Violent Crime Control and Law Enforcement Act, which cut off these grants. The reasoning for this was simple: people wanted to know why prisoners should get free education when those who are not jailed are required to pay for it. The act's passage had an instant impact behind bars. "Immediately programs began to shut down," wrote Martin, "they are now all but gone." This was part of an effort, added Martin, "in a more conservative direction. . . . The idea that it should be a concern of society to help prisoners better themselves disappeared; instead, prison became a place where people were thrown away to pay for their crimes."

In 2007, Congress changed direction once again and passed the Second Chance Act of 2007. This law provides funding for new education programs in prisons, and was enacted to help improve recidivism rates. Over the past two decades, studies have shown that inmates who improve their education while in prison are less likely to be rearrested. In one study of more than three thousand inmates in Maryland, Ohio, and Minnesota, only 21 percent of those who participated in education programs were incarcerated again, compared to 31 percent who did not enroll in these programs.

Max Kenner, director of the Bard Prison Initiative in New York, said, "Those who participate in higher education in prison are less likely to go back and less likely to fail in the workplace." They realize that an education gives them a better chance to support themselves in the community and stay out of prison.

According to another study conducted in 2007, even completion of a high school program can help inmates find jobs once they are released. Not only do inmates improve their skills, but they also show potential employers that they are serious about making an effort to find a steady job.

During the first decade of the twenty-first century, many states offered high school diploma programs or general education development certificate programs, in addition to higher education, to inmates. In North Carolina, the state Department of Correction, together with the North Carolina Community College system, enabled about one-third of all inmates to take college courses annually. They could even finish their degrees once they were released from prison by utilizing partnership opportunities offered by community colleges and universities. Boston University, along with Partakers, a nonprofit organization, has worked to provide college courses for inmates in Massachusetts, called the College Behind Bars Program. The program also includes mentoring for individual students by faculty members. Lanny Kutakoff, director of the program, said, "We discovered [that] having this kind of relationship profoundly impacts students' grades and retention rates."

Nevertheless, since states have needed to cut their budgets, some prison education programs have suffered. In California, for example, the state took $250 million out of the program and laid off nine hundred teachers. Cindie Fonesca, one of the teachers who lost her job, said, "They're going to learn from their 'cellies' [other prisoners]. That's what they're going to do . . . how to be better criminals." But then, governor Arnold Schwarzenegger said that economic realities have forced the budget cuts. "You cannot pay out the same amount to prisons. We cannot pay out the same amount to education, to in-home support services, to any of those things. Everyone has to cut back."

The cutbacks in prison funding do not bother many people. In fact, a 2010 survey conducted by the Public Policy Institute of California found that only 11 percent of California residents would be willing to pay higher taxes to maintain the current level of funding for prisons. By comparison, some 66 percent said they would be willing to pay higher taxes to do the same thing for K-12 education. Fifty-eight percent of those polled said they would like to see education spared from any future budget cuts, but only 6 percent said they would like to see prisons spared.

5 Prison Violence

"WE HAVE A POLICY OF ENGAGEMENT, AND I THINK it's working," said New York City police commissioner Raymond Kelly. The commissioner was referring to the fact that the homicide rate in New York had dropped by more than 10 percent since 2008, reaching its lowest level in forty-plus years. Homicide rates also have dropped in other large cities, such as Los Angeles, Atlanta, and Chicago. Part of the reason is good police work. In New York, police put extra patrols in neighborhoods that seem at greatest risk for crime. They also stop and frisk people who appear suspicious and may be carrying a gun. The rates of other major crimes, like robbery and auto theft, also have declined.

Norman Seabrook, president of the Correction Officers' Benevolent Association, believes he knows why the crime rates have declined so dramatically. It is because more people are locked up than ever before. In 2005, Seabrook wrote, "Politicians boast that they are keeping the streets safer than ever, which logically follows since more offenders are being placed behind bars."

It is likely that the problem of violence may only have shifted from America's streets to its prisons. As states face increasing budget deficits, they have been unable to raise their expenditures for correctional institutions. Prisons are overcrowded, Seabrook wrote in 2005, with statistics from seventeen states showing a 5 percent or higher increase in the number of inmates in recent years. Meanwhile, the number of correctional officers who must oversee the

Prisons are violent places and gangs flourish inside their walls.

prisoners has remained the same or declined frequently. At the same time, violent assaults by one prisoner against another have risen by 27 percent, while assaults against correctional officers are 32 percent higher, Seabrook wrote.

Hearing about the rising number of violent incidents in prison does not bother many Americans. In fact, the use of violence in general does not seem to bother most Americans. Sasha Abramsky, an author who has written several books on the subject of prisons, discusses this subject in detail in his book, *American Furies: Crime, Punishment, and Vengeance in the Age of Mass Imprisonment.* Abramsky wrote: "The United States has a far higher rate of violent crime than other first world democracies . . . as the violence embedded in the laws of many other countries has ebbed, the worst aspects of the American incarceration experience have been allowed to flower. Beatings and gassings, racial harassment, sexual abuse, the catastrophic maltreatment of the mentally ill, and the use of solitary confinement as a punishment tool are all . . . mainstays of the modern correctional system. . . . [O]nce the doors to the prison click shut, the conditions inside are out of sight, out of mind to the rest of the population."

A Bureau of Justice Statistics survey conducted in 2007 reported that more than 60,000 inmates—or about 4.5 percent of the U.S. prison population at the time the survey was conducted—had reported incidents of sexual violence. These incidents include rape, touching, and other unwanted sexual advances by one inmate against another or by a correctional officer against an inmate. The survey showed that sexual violence has continued, even since the passage of the Prison Rape Elimination Act in 2003 set a "zero-tolerance standard" for rape and ordered the Department of Justice to "make the prevention of prison rape a top priority in each prison system." States that fail to comply could see their federal funding slashed.

Since that time, there has been progress in dealing with sexual violence in prison. The National Institute of Corrections has conducted workshops for correctional officers, and training programs have been instituted at prisons across the United States. Ohio is one state that has adopted such a program, and correctional administrators there have reported an "overall change in tone" as a result.

A majority of states have staff training programs, as well as periodic refresher courses to review the training principles. Corrections officers learn how to detect possible perpetrators of sexual violence, both inmates and staff members; how to identify possible victims; and how to conduct incident investigations, protect the safety of inmates under their care, and discipline those who are guilty of sexual violence.

In addition, states offer educational programs to inmates regarding sexual violence when they are processed at selection centers. These include information about the Prison Rape Elimination Act, their rights as victims, how to report incidents, and how to prevent rape by another inmate or member of the staff.

Nevertheless, a 2006 study of the Texas prison system revealed that incidents of rape continue. Indeed, Texas has the highest rate in the United States. The study showed that a majority of victims are white, younger than their attackers, and suffering from mental health problems. Potential victims are supposed to be identified in the state screening process during intake and offered protection. Nevertheless, overcrowding and a reduced officer-to-inmate ratio have made this impossible in many cases.

Many victims are women. In the 2009 report by the National Prison Rape Elimination Commission, former inmate Necole Brown revealed in an interview, "I continue to contend with flash-backs of what this correctional officer did to me and the guilt, shame, and rage that comes with having been sexually violated for so many years." Tom Cahill, who spent only one night in a jail in San Antonio, Texas, reported that after being gang-raped, "I've been hospitalized more times than I can count and I didn't pay for those hospitalizations, the taxpayers paid. My career as a journalist and photographer was completely derailed."

The commission reported that rates of sexual abuse varied greatly, with 15.7 percent of prisoners in one facility reporting abuse. Some of them reported being attacked by other inmates, while even more reported being attacked by staff members. The commission called for mandatory criminal background checks of potential staff members to identify those who may commit sexual crimes. Prisoners also needed educational programs "about their right to be safe and the facility's commitment to holding all perpetrators of sexual abuse—staff and inmates—accountable." In addition, prison systems need better screening to identify prisoners who might be at risk.

These include inmates with mental health problems, women, and small prisoners who can be easily overpowered. They also need to be protected by being placed in cells with few roommates. "When Timothy Taylor was incarcerated in a Michigan prison," the commission reported, "internal assessments suggested that he was likely to be a target of sexual abuse because of his small size—he was 5 feet tall and 120 pounds—and diminished mental abilities, yet he was placed in a prison dormitory to save bed space for new arrivals. Shortly thereafter, he was sexually assaulted by another prisoner."

Overcrowding and lack of staff have made protection for prisoners far more difficult. Many prisoners are also unwilling to report sexual abuse. They fear being "bullied into silence and harmed if they speak out," reported the commission. They also believe that some members of the staff will not pay attention to them. Inmate Cyryna Pasion told the commissioners, "When I told one of the guards I trusted how tired I was of putting up with abuse, he told me to just ignore it." Staff also are untrained in conducting investigations of sexual abuse, and only a small number of those accused of abuse are prosecuted. In addition, the victims frequently do not receive counseling after an incident, nor do they receive HIV testing. Michael Blucker entered a correctional center in Illinois with no indication of HIV, but a year after his incarceration and after being victimized by rape, he had contracted the disease.

Violence or the potential for violence are facts of life for women as well as men. Marianne McNabb, a private criminal justice consultant to various private and state agencies, interviewed women between 2007 and 2008 and discovered that they "do not consider either jails or prisons to be safe places." Violence may begin as verbal abuse and continue in more harmful forms. One of the reasons is that the intake procedures are not sufficient to prevent highly vulnerable women from being placed in cells with those who might bully them.

Inmates earn small amounts of money—sometimes as little as twelve cents an hour—for the work that they are assigned to do in prison. They use their wages to buy items from the prison store, and also to pay restitution to those they have committed crimes against, if they have been ruled to do so. But with little money available to them, especially if no one from outside the prison is sending them money, they often borrow from other inmates and go into debt. This makes them vulnerable to pressure that may lead to physical violence if the debts are not repaid. Some women try to earn money by making themselves available to staff members for sexual favors. McNabb suggests the correctional facilities provide better training for staff members regarding policies prohibiting sexual violence. One way to do this might be to frequently remind staff members of prison policies regarding exploitation of inmates. In addition, women prisoners should be given reassurance that if they report incidents, something will be done about them.

McNabb said many women prisoners, beginning at a young age, have experienced victimization, violence, and trauma, including both physical and sexual trauma. Many women also have a history of substance abuse, poor family relationships, and economic hardship. As a result, inmates may come to rely on other inmates as part of an extended family. Therefore, prison staff must ensure that, as much as possible, these relationships are not abusive. If incidents do occur, women need to receive counseling from professionals who understand the needs of female inmates. McNabb concluded, "The good news is that safety for women in jail's [sic] and prisons has improved. . . . The response to the Prison Rape Elimination Act on the part of correctional administrators and policy makers has meant a serious realignment of priorities and resources." She added that policies and sanctions regarding staff sexual misconduct reportedly had curtailed the most obvious cases of such behavior.

Violence and Corrections Officers

Many corrections officers fear they will become targets of violence committed by prisoners. The numbers support their fear. In 1995, one report submitted to the Department of Justice said there were more than 14,000 reported attacks on corrections officers by inmates, using weapons such as broken glass, safety razors, and sharpened toothbrushes. The assaults led to the death of fourteen staff members. Just five years later, there were roughly 18,000 attacks on corrections officers.

This potential for violence is a major cause of stress among prison staff. "In the pod, there's no getting away from the inmates,"

Direct
Supervision
Correctional
Facilities

Office West works in a pod, part of the design of a direct supervision correctional facility. These institutions began to appear in the 1970s in New York City, San Diego, and Chicago as part of the federal prison system. They differed from the traditional prison design that consisted of cells along long hallways that were patrolled periodically by correctional officers. As authors Christine Tartaro and Marissa Levy wrote in *American Jails* magazine, "An obvious problem with intermittent supervision is that inmates have until the officer's next patrol to assault cellmates or commit other types of infractions."

In the direct supervision facility—there were approximately three hundred of them in 2009—cells are built around a dayroom where inmates have recreational activities, educational programs, and meals. The correctional officer interacts with the prisoners directly—a ratio of one officer to about sixty prisoners is common. Each pod is relatively independent, and officers provide services to the inmates in their pod. If an officer spots a problem with an inmate or recognizes that a conflict may be about to occur between inmates, he or she is expected to step in and diffuse the situation. After the activities are completed, the prisoners return to their cells, which can be easily observed by an officer in the dayroom.

Studies suggest various benefits to the direct supervision approach. Relations between officers and inmates are more positive because they interact more often. There is also less violence among inmates and against correctional staff members. But to be successful in a direct supervision facility, officers need to receive training in communications skills and interpersonal relationships, especially if they need to diffuse a potentially violent situation. Yet many facilities provide an average of only two days' training in communication to their officers. In addition, overcrowding can make an officer's job far more difficult.

Corrections Officer Lou West told the Commission on Safety and Abuse in America's Prisons. "I'm asked to address all their needs and to be ready for any emotional disturbance." West is in charge of sixty-seven inmates.

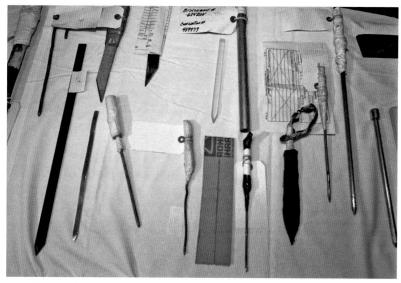

Drug deals and the violence that often goes along with them don't stop when the dealers are incarcerated. A raid in a Pennsylvania prison turned up an enormous cache of weapons, including these items.

The job of a correctional officer has become more difficult as inmate populations have increased. Thus, additional training has become necessary. Theodis Beck, secretary of the North Carolina Department of Correction, explained, "Today's correctional officer must be able to look at situations from an inmate's perspective. He must be in tune to the changing situation of aging inmates, know how to deal with offenders who may be suicidal, be able to recognize gang signs and colors, speak foreign languages, and be sensitive to issues involving supervision of offenders of the opposite sex."

For example, gangs may flourish inside a correctional facility. In 2005, a gang inside the Bayside Correctional Facility in New Jersey initiated a violent uprising that injured twenty-nine correctional officers before it was finally brought under control. Officers later testified before New Jersey's Assembly Prison Gang Violence Task Force that they had received little or no training in "how to identify gang members, what their gang signs and nicknames are, how they move and with whom they associate." Officers also did not know how to deal with a major threat inside a prison. The task force recommended that all staff should receive at least sixteen hours of gang training, and also learn how to deal with riots as well as how to stop the flow of all types of contraband. Officers also needed to be made aware of information about gangs that was being collected by the Department of Corrections' Special Investigations Division, which provides assistance with intelligence and investigations to law enforcement agencies of all levels.

A correctional officer's job can be extremely stressful. In some prisons, a single officer is responsible for supervising as many as one hundred inmates. A major part of the stress occurs because many of these prisoners are violent. They may threaten a correctional officer at any time. Weapons are presumably unavailable to inmates; nevertheless, some gain possession of them. They may fashion a safety razor into a weapon, file down a toothbrush until it becomes dangerous, or attach a blade to the end of a toothbrush.

In 2009, *American Jails* cited a study that said, "Attacks on property or persons within the facility are common because inmates are bored and frustrated, and they may threaten, or become verbally/physically assaultive to other inmates and staff. . . . [I]nmates use violence as a way to feel self-important due to interpersonal failures." Prisons often do not provide sufficient counseling and educational programs to deal with these issues. In addition, officers' stress may arise from sources outside their job sites. Some studies have pointed out that since correctional officers often are portrayed as brutes in the news and popular media they sometimes distance themselves from those close to them on a personal level, such as family.

The effects of stress vary among correctional staff. As is the case in many other occupations, some staff members suffer from high blood pressure and heart disease, while others develop anger management problems and express their anger against inmates or family members. Still others suffer from drug abuse problems.

Problems exist in all correctional systems, including federal ones. On June 20, 2008, for example, Corrections Officer Jose Rivera was stabbed to death by two prisoners at the U.S. Penitentiary in Atwater, California. The federal system, which includes Atwater, was short-staffed during that time period, while inmate crowding raised the prison population to 37 percent above capacity. At the same time, violence against corrections officers increased, up 6 percent from 2005. This suggested there may be a relationship between overcrowding and violence.

Testifying in front of the U.S. House of Representatives, Bryan Lowry, president of the American Federation of Government Employees' Council of Prison Locals, pointed out, "High security penitentiaries currently assign only one correctional officer to each housing unit. This unsound correctional practice is particularly dangerous during the evening watch shift when only one officer is available to perform the 4:00 p.m. inmate count and the 11:00 p.m. inmate lockup." Correctional Officer Rivera was alone locking inmates into the cells for the 4 p.m. inmate count when he was murdered. In 2008, the Bureau of Prisons assigned another staff member to high-security facilities for the evening shifts. In addition, the Bureau of Prisons has decided to make available to all correctional officers protective vests that enable officers to resist stab wounds.

Lowry also called on the Bureau of Prisons to step up its inmate work program. Congress had cut funding to this program during the first decade of the twenty-first century as a cost-savings measure. Nevertheless, studies have shown that the program helped prevent boredom among the prisoners, and the violence that could result from it. The program also instilled work values and enabled prisoners to learn important skills. Those who were employed by the program also were 35 percent less likely to return to prison during the first twelve months after their release because many of them could find jobs in the community. All of these measures have the potential to reduce stress for correctional officers and improve their safety as they work in prisons.

By no means are inmates the only ones guilty of committing violence behind bars. Often, corrections officers are charged with abuse. In June 2010, for example, a former corrections officer at California's Chino State Prison was sentenced to more than four years in prison for abusing inmates in a 2002 incident. He had thrown shackled inmates to the ground and conspired to cover it up. Similar claims of abuse—frequently of a sexual nature—turn up in newspaper headlines on a regular basis.

Guards worry about violent action against them, but they are also guilty of violence against prisoners. This image from a video shows a prisoner with a broken ankle being dragged from his cell at the Brazoria County Detention Center in Texas.

6 Juvenile Inmates

IN 2008, COLTON HARRIS-MOORE—WIDELY KNOWN as the Barefoot Bandit—escaped from a juvenile detention center in Washington State. For roughly the next two years until he was caught in July 2010, he engaged in a burglary spree that included breaking into homes and stores and stealing boats and airplanes. He has been described as a "teen Jesse James," and has more than one fan page on Facebook, the most popular of which boasts 35,000 fans. As he was growing up, theft became "a survival mechanism" for Harris-Moore, said Robin Lowell, who knew Colton's family.

The Harris-Moore case was an exceptional one that gathered news coverage from across the world. But of course he was not the only juvenile incarcerated in the United States. According to the most recent data available, in 2006, more than 92,800 juveniles—usually defined as youths under eighteen years old—were placed in detention centers nationwide. Juvenile detention centers are similar to jails and prisons. About one-third of those in detention centers were being detained until a judge could hear their case, while the rest already had been sentenced for committing a crime. Among those in detention, about 31,000 had committed offenses such as homicide, assault, or robbery. More than 20,000 were placed in a facility because of crimes such as auto theft and arson, while another 8,000 had committed crimes involving the possession or sale of drugs. Some juveniles are placed in detention

Defense attorney Daniel Bagdade talks with Nathaniel Jamal Abraham, twelve, of Pontiac, Michigan, in juvenile court on Feb. 11, 1998. Abraham was eleven when charged with first-degree murder in the shooting of an eighteen-year-old stranger outside a convenience store. He was the youngest person ever to be convicted of murder. He was sentenced as a juvenile and, a year after being released, was arrested on a drug charge.

facilities because of "status offenses." These are offenses, such as repeatedly running away from home or not attending school, that are not typically thought of as crimes.

Although they make up a minority of the juvenile population in the United States, African American and Hispanic youths comprise a majority of those in correctional facilities. Of every 100,000 juveniles, about 170 whites are in a detention center, compared to 767 African Americans. Sixty-five percent of robberies and more than 40 percent of homicides committed by juveniles are by African Americans.

Many reports have been issued in an attempt to determine the reasons for such glaring racial discrepancies. One prepared in 2009 by the Criminal Justice Program of the National Conference of State Legislatures said those explanations range from "jurisdictional issues, certain police practices and punitive juvenile crime legislation of the 1990s to perceived racial bias in the system." The report offered further explanation on each of these four topics:

- Jurisdictional issues—Cases tried in urban areas, where minority populations are concentrated, are more likely to result in harsher outcomes than similar cases in nonurban areas where more whites are located. Also, urban crimes tend to be more visible to law enforcement than nonurban ones.
- Certain police practices—Many police practices target low-income urban neighborhoods where minorities live.
- Punitive juvenile laws—Tough laws that have made it easier to try youths as adults for certain crimes have disproportionately impacted minority youths.
- Perceived racial bias—Several studies conducted by the Office of Juvenile Justice and Delinquency Prevention have shown that "negative race effects" were present at various stages of the criminal justice system.

Nationally, about 15 percent of juveniles in detention facilities are females, a figure that has risen over the past decade. More girls are committing violent crimes such as assault and murder. They also account for more than 25 percent of the 1.7 million delinquency cases handled by juvenile courts annually. This figure has risen from 400,000 in 1960. Juvenile delinquency usually is defined as a legal violation that has been committed by a youth age seventeen or younger. Many factors have been cited for the rising number of girls getting in trouble with the law, including zero-tolerance policies in schools and the increase in girls being initiated into gangs.

Gang members are involved in a large number of serious crimes, such as robberies and assaults. They and other juveniles may be sent to a detention center run by the state or a private company. About one-third of all juvenile detainees are in private facilities. These youths are primarily those who have committed minor offenses, such as petty theft. Those who have committed more serious crimes are generally in state-operated correctional centers. Overall, detention of youth has risen by almost 50 percent between 1985 and 2005—part of an effort to get tough on criminals of all ages.

Juveniles in the Court System

During the early part of the nineteenth century, youths accused of crime were treated just like adults. They were given harsh sentences, locked away in adult prisons, and sometimes even hanged for their crimes. But changes occurred by the middle part of the nineteenth century as reformers led a successful effort to treat children differently from adults. They persuaded political leaders that many youths accused of crimes had come from impoverished homes and turned to robbery or some other form of crime as a way to survive. Detention centers, called reform schools, that were dedicated to house only juvenile offenders soon opened. These reform schools were designed to reform delinquent youths, train them in vocational skills, and eventually return them to the community after completion of their sentence.

In 1899, Chicago became the first city to begin a juvenile justice system. By 1925, almost every state had a juvenile court system. In juvenile court, the rules were quite different from the adult court system. There were no juries; instead, judges heard the cases brought against juveniles and made a decision. In juvenile court, a youth was never considered guilty of a crime; instead, he or she was "adjudicated delinquent." Many of these youths were returned to the community on probation, and under the authority of a probation officer. Others were sent to reform schools to serve out their sentences.

But problems soon arose in these institutions. Younger delinquents sometimes fell prey to older youths who physically and sexually abused them. Due to this and other reasons, reform schools proved to be an ineffective way to rehabilitate youths, and many children remained in institutions for long sentences. So, by the end of the twentieth century, the courts were making every effort to keep juveniles out of reform schools and place them in the community. They might be sent to group homes or shelters—residential homes where people who share common characteristics live—where they lived in the community and were carefully monitored by shelter staff as well as probation officers.

Beginning in the 1960s, Congress passed a series of laws designed to more effectively safeguard the rights of juveniles in the justice system. Under the Juvenile Justice and Delinquency Prevention Act of 1974, Congress ordered that any juveniles who had committed status offenses should not be placed in correctional facilities. In 1980, Congress amended the act, stating that juveniles could not be placed in the same cells as adults while awaiting appearances in court.

When a case is referred to juvenile court, it is evaluated by an intake officer or a prosecutor, depending on the way the particular court is structured. The officer or prosecutor looks at the evidence and decides whether the case should proceed. Some cases are dismissed due to lack of evidence. About half the cases are "handled informally," as stated in the Juvenile Offenders and Victims: 2006 National Report. In many of these cases, juveniles who basically have admitted their guilt agree to perform certain types of activities under an agreement known as a consent decree. These activities may include drug counseling or community service. If the juvenile carries out these responsibilities, the case will be dismissed.

Other cases proceed to court where the juvenile's lawyer and the lawyer prosecuting the case argue its merits in front of a judge. Witnesses appear to testify in the case, and then the judge considers the

Juvenile Delinquents and the U.S. Supreme Court

The U.S. Supreme Court has made several rulings that had an important impact on the rights of juveniles. One of these rulings involved the case of twelve-year-old Samuel Winship, who was accused of stealing $112 from a woman's handbag. Winship was adjudicated delinquent based on the "preponderance of the evidence." This was standard in juvenile courts at the time, rather than "proof beyond a reasonable doubt," which was the standard under the U.S. Constitution for adult defendants. In 1970, the Supreme Court ruled (*In re Winship*) that juvenile courts should use the same, higher standard of "proof beyond a reasonable doubt" for juveniles.

In a vast majority of jurisdictions, juvenile courts do not have jury trials, thanks to a ruling by the U.S. Supreme Court. That leaves decisions up to the judge based on the evidence presented in a case. When sixteen-year-old Joseph McKeiver was accused of robbery and larceny in 1968, his lawyer asked for a jury trial. The request was denied, and McKeiver was placed on probation by the judge in the case. McKeiver's lawyers appealed, and the case reached the Supreme Court. In *McKeiver* v. *Pennsylvania* (1971), the Supreme Court ruled that a jury was unnecessary in juvenile courts because, in part, juries are not known to be more accurate than judges.

In 1977, Gregory Martin, then fourteen, was charged with robbery and assault on another boy and held in detention. When a youth is accused of a serious crime, he may be held in detention pending his appearance in court if he is considered a "serious risk" to the community. Martin's lawyer challenged this decision, stating that it was a violation of a fundamental right under the U.S. Constitution—a defendant cannot be punished without a trial. Detention, the lawyer argued, was punishment because most defendants were released while awaiting their court appearances. In *Schall* v. *Martin* (1984), the U.S. Supreme Court disagreed, explaining that preventive detention serves to protect both the juvenile and society from pretrial crime and is not intended as a means of punishment.

In more recent crime-related cases of juveniles, the Supreme Court has ruled that neither the death penalty nor life sentences may be levied against juveniles.

evidence and makes a final decision. During the proceedings, the juvenile may be required to remain in a detention center. In the final decision, many defendants are ordered to serve probation, a supervision program in which the offender must complete certain requirements such as meeting a curfew or attending certain programs. In addition, they may be required to have counseling and even to report to a detention center on weekends. In roughly 25 percent of the cases, the juvenile is ordered by the judge to confinement in a juvenile detention center for a specific prison term. These cases involve serious offenses such as murder, rape, and robbery.

Juvenile Detention Facilities

Juvenile detention facilities vary by the conditions under which juveniles are confined. In state-run facilities, more than half are "locked." That is, youths are locked in their rooms at night for sleeping, or they may be sent to locked rooms when they cause a disturbance. In addition, these facilities often have security fences around them and locked gates. Approximately 7 percent of youths confined to privately run detention centers are in locked facilities. Youths judged delinquent for serious offenses are generally placed in locked detention facilities.

Other facilities are "staff secure." That is, staff members provide security instead of using locks to confine juveniles. These facilities generally serve youths judged delinquent for less serious crimes, such as minor drug and alcohol violations. Staff-secure facilities include wilderness camps, group homes, and boot camps. Overcrowding is a problem at all juvenile facilities, especially larger detention centers with over one hundred residents. Approximately 15 to 20 percent of these facilities run over capacity.

Most juveniles in residential facilities are age twelve and older. In 2006, there were only about 1,200 youths under age twelve in detention centers. In Wisconsin, for example, youths twelve and older can be placed in secured juvenile correctional institutions.

Those who have committed serious crimes may receive sentences of five years or more. If that sentence lasts past the offender's eighteenth birthday, he or she can be transferred to an adult facility. During a brief orientation, staff members talk to juveniles, explain the rules, and provide them with any other information they need. They are screened by a staff that includes social workers, youth counselors, and mental health experts. For example, when juveniles enter a detention facility in Wisconsin, they are routinely tested to determine whether they have problems with drugs or alcohol, or whether they require mental health counseling. In that state, any juveniles who have not yet graduated from high school also are required to attend school at the facility. A variety of mandatory treatment programs also are available, including drug and alcohol counseling, anger management, vocational training, and computer courses. Other states offer similar programs.

Problems in Juvenile Detention Centers

Despite efforts by Wisconsin and other states to reform and rehabilitate juvenile delinquents, many problems have been reported in detention facilities. In 2008, Mississippi decided to close the Columbia Training School—a facility for juveniles, many of whom were runaways from abusive homes. The staff allegedly had abused juvenile inmates. Ashley Fantz, a reporter for CNN, interviewed an inmate named Erica, who said she was chained and handcuffed when she had meals or went to the bathroom. Fantz also quoted a note written by a fifteen-year-old girl who alleged she had been sexually abused by a facility staff member. Meanwhile, in Florida, there have been seven deaths among juvenile inmates since 2000. And Texas has fired or disciplined ninety staff members during the same period for sexual abuse.

Another report by the Justice Department stated that more than four thousand juveniles in correctional facilities, or about 17 per 1,000, were sexually abused by staff members or other inmates between 2005 and 2006. Inmates who abuse or attack other inmates are often admired by the rest of the juvenile prisoners, according to the report.

The National Prison Rape Elimination Commission Report of 2009 stated, "Juveniles in confinement are much more likely than incarcerated adults to be sexually abused." While the rate of sexual abuse in adult facilities is about 2.9 per thousand, the rate in juvenile facilities is 16.8 per thousand. In a juvenile facility in Indiana, youths as young as twelve years old were sexually abused by older teenagers. Children weighing as little as seventy pounds were being abused by those outweighing them by one hundred pounds or more. The smaller kids had little chance of fending off the older inmates. Girls in juvenile institutions comprised over one-third of those victimized by rape, although they were only about 15 percent of the inmate population.

There also have been reports of problems in boot camps for juvenile delinquents. These are programs that often take place in wilderness areas where youths are required to submit to strict military discipline during their sentence in an attempt to reform their behavior. As reported by the Government Accountability Office, a watchdog agency of the federal government, these programs serve between 10,000 and 20,000 youths at a cost of about $130 to $450 per day—money that ultimately comes from taxpayers. Over the years, the Government Accountability Office has investigated several deaths of youths who were placed in these programs. One of these was sixteen-year-old Aaron Bacon, who had been sent to boot camp in 1994 after he was found to be using drugs in school. According to Aaron's father, Bob, the teen spent fourteen days with little food and was required to take daily hikes of about eight to ten miles. Bob Bacon said, "On the days he did have food, it consisted of undercooked lentils, lizards, scorpions, trail mix and a celebrated canned peach on the thirteenth day." Aaron Bacon ended up dying while at boot camp.

Prosecutor Pam Bondi shows a video during court proceedings on Oct. 3, 2007, in Panama City, Florida, where seven former juvenile boot camp guards and a nurse were on trial for the death of an African-American teenager in January 2006.

In 2008, reporter Seamus McGraw wrote about fourteen-year-old Tony Haynes, who been sent to boot camp after being arrested for shoplifting. Haynes, according to witnesses, wanted to leave the program and was punished for this by being forced to sit out in temperatures that reached 110°F (43°C), with no water. Soon afterward, he died. Other young people, however, have found the camps beneficial. Pedro Madrid, according to his mother, changed his entire life as a result of an experience at boot camp. Nevertheless, thirty-five juveniles have died in boot camps since 1983, and others have suffered broken bones. Researchers also point out that the recidivism rate at boot camps—about 49 percent—is about the same as it is in other types of correctional facilities.

A study of New York juvenile detention released in 2009 by the U.S. Department of Justice revealed that "Excessive physical force was routinely used to discipline children at several juvenile prisons . . . resulting in broken bones, shattered teeth, concussions and dozens of other serious injuries . . . " The report added, "Anything from sneaking an extra cookie to initiating a fist fight may result in a full prone restraint with handcuffs. This one-size-fits-all approach has, not surprisingly, led to an alarming number of serious injuries to youth[s]." The report went on to point out that force violated the inmates' constitutional rights against "cruel and unusual punishment."

Juveniles Confined in Adult Facilities

During the past two decades, public opinion has supported harsher punishment for juveniles who are guilty of very serious crimes. In twenty-three states, there is no minimum age for transferring a juvenile to criminal court and trying the offender as an adult. For other states the minimum age is fourteen, and for two, Kansas and Vermont, the minimum age is ten. Approximately 8,500 youths under age eighteen are confined in adult correctional institutions. These juveniles are at greater risk for physical abuse and sexual assault from the typically larger and stronger adult inmates.

An increasing number of juveniles also have been sentenced to life in prison without parole for crimes such as murder. Human Rights Watch, a leading human rights organization, reported that more than two thousand juveniles were in prison for life sentences. "Criminal punishment in the United States can serve four goals," the organization said, "rehabilitation, retribution, deterrence and incapacitation. . . . Sentencing children to life without parole fails to measure up on all counts." Many such prisoners were less than sixteen years old when they were sentenced. While many were murderers, others had simply been "participants in a robbery or burglary in which a murder was committed by someone else." Only thirteen other nations in the world impose such life sentences on juveniles.

However, many people believe the old adage "an eye for an eye" should apply to all criminals, regardless of age. In 2009, New York

Mental Health
Needs of
Juvenile
Offenders

As a result of the 2008 economic recession, many states reduced their expenditures for mental health counseling in towns, cities, and schools. Instead, states relied more heavily on juvenile detention centers to deal with young people whose mental health problems may have resulted in criminal activities. "We're seeing more and more mentally ill kids who couldn't find community programs that were intensive enough to treat them," said Joseph Penn, director of mental health services for the University of Texas Medical Branch Correctional Managed Care. "Jails and juvenile justice facilities are the new asylums." Inmates also sometimes receive medication with little or no counseling to go along with it.

The situation is especially serious in California. In Los Angeles County, for example, Dr. Eric Trupin, a psychologist and consultant for the correctional system, pointed out that "some detainees appeared to be held there for no reason other than that they were mentally ill and the county had no other institution capable of treating them."

The mental health staff members who try to help juvenile inmates may have very little information about them. Many of the inmates come from families that are not intact, and school records may not accompany an inmate to a correctional facility.

State representative William Snyder told the *New York Times* why he believes this should be the case. "Sometimes a 15-year-old has a tremendous appreciation for right and wrong," he said. "I think it would be wrong for the Supreme Court to say that it was patently illegal or improper to send a youthful offender to life without parole. At a certain point, juveniles cross the line, and they have to be treated as adults and punished as adults."

Nevertheless, states across America are currently examining their juvenile facilities and urging improvements. In Nebraska, for example, a 2007 report called for expanding services to youths who "have behavioral disorders, mental heath [sic], substance abuse, and sex offender treatment needs, and also called for increases in staffing to create a ratio of one staff member to eight inmates because," the report says, it "reflects a staffing pattern that is appropriate for intensive therapeutic programming." Other jurisdictions are trying to create alternatives to detention. For example, Berks County, Pennsylvania, has established an evening reporting center in an area of high juvenile crime. This is an alternative to detention while juveniles are waiting for court appearances. The center provides counseling, help with homework, recreation, and more. All juveniles have reported regularly to the center in the evenings and only one has been involved in a new crime in that time span.

7 The Immigrant Detention System

THE T. DON HUTTO RESIDENTIAL CENTER IN TAYLOR, Texas, was, until 2009, one of two immigrant detention facilities in America that housed families. Hutto, as it is called, is run by the Corrections Corporation of America, a prison management company started in 1983. It is one of several private companies that run prisons used by the Department of Homeland Security to house immigrants. Some of these immigrants have entered the United States illegally; others who seek asylum are being held while their cases are being heard; still others are incarcerated for committing crimes. Since many immigrants have children, Congress decided that if parents were held in custody, their children would be separated from them without anywhere to live. The Department of Homeland Security—as reported by Margaret Talbot, a *New Yorker* writer who did an in-depth piece in 2008 on children housed in immigrant detention facilities—could have decided to release the immigrants into the community. They might have been required to wear electronic ankle bracelets so authorities could keep track of them. This would have been less expensive. Instead, the Department of Homeland Security decided to incarcerate them in facilities like Hutto.

Talbot's article relates the plight of several families, including that of Salwan Komo, his wife, Neven, and their infant daughter. The Komos were refugees from Iraq who came to the United States seeking asylum, or protection, from Muslim guerrillas who threat-

A group of Mexican immigrants await processing in a U.S. Border Patrol detention center in Nogales, Arizona.

ened the small Christian minority to which they belonged. Instead of receiving asylum, however, the Komos were stopped by the U.S. Immigration and Customs Enforcement Division (ICE) of the Department of Homeland Security when they entered North America, and were placed in the Hutto detention center. The family was released after a short stay and given asylum.

A 2009 report by The Constitution Project, a research organization, revealed that 300,000 immigrants are held in detention by the U.S. government each year. This is an increase of approximately 40 percent since 2003. After the terrorist attacks of September 11,

2001, the Department of Homeland Security began rounding up people who had entered the United States illegally, out of fear that they might be involved in a terrorist plot.

As a result, approximately 33,000 undocumented immigrants are incarcerated every day, and are held in more than five hundred detention facilities. The Federal Bureau of Prisons lacked the space in its correctional centers to incarcerate all of these people. So some are held in jails, some in state prisons, and still others are held in privately run correctional centers. While the average length of stay for any prisoner is about thirty-seven days, some have remained in detention for several years. If they cannot afford lawyers to help them with their cases, the immigrants receive no legal counsel—unlike American citizens who have a right to legal representation under the U.S. Constitution.

Living conditions at immigrant detention facilities are dreadful. Women and children live together, while fathers must live separately. The Yourdkhanis, refugees from Iran, were another family that was arrested and placed in Hutto. Majid Yourdkhani was forced to stay in a separate cell from his wife and daughter; and, when he became ill, his wife could not help him. Children at Hutto were forced to wear striped suits, and were given neither toys nor something as simple as paper and crayons to pass the time. Families were forced to awake at 5:30 a.m., and throughout the night lights were shone into their cells, making it difficult for anyone to sleep. Children also were disciplined by the staff for running around and yelling—basically, for behaving like children.

In 2007, the American Civil Liberties Union (ACLU), an organization that defends civil rights, sued the Department of Homeland Security over conditions at Hutto. An investigation conducted as part of the lawsuit found that children were forced to live in an environment that was "capable of contributing to the development of unnecessary anxiety and stress [for them]." As a result of the suit, Homeland Security agreed to improve conditions at Hutto.

Children were given pajamas to sleep in and toys to play with, and school instruction was increased to seven hours a day from only an hour. In 2009, Hutto became a facility for adult women only.

However, unpleasant conditions remain in other detention facilities. The Constitution Project reported that these centers suffer from overcrowding, and "two or three detainees must sleep in cells intended to hold one person." Health care is inadequate, children receive no education or recreation, and some of those detained for illegally entering the United States or seeking asylum are put in cells with those who have committed crimes. "This practice puts immigration detainees at risk of physical harm, and many report the occurrence of threats, confrontations, and physical violence between them and their criminal counterparts."

In January 2010, the *New York Times* reported that, since 2003, 107 immigrants had died while in detention. The article noted that, as stated in an investigation conducted by a federal agency, "unbearable, untreated pain had been a significant factor in the suicide" of one detainee, Nery Romero from El Salvador. The investigation found that the staff of the detention center had covered up this problem by making a "fake entry" that said Romero had been given a painkiller. Romero died in a jail in Bergen County, New Jersey, although a spokesman for that facility would not say whether any changes had been made since the death. At another center, Boubacar Bah, a tailor from Guinea in Africa, suffered a fractured skull, the cause of which was not reported. For thirteen hours, no one called for an ambulance. Bah eventually was taken to a hospital where emergency surgery was performed, but he died anyway.

A 2009 report by Human Rights Watch concluded that the medical care in immigrant detention centers was dangerously inadequate, and stated, "Women in detention described violations such as shackling pregnant detainees or failing to follow up on signs of breast and cervical cancer, as well as basic affronts to their dignity." Effective medical treatment often was delayed, and some women were prevented from receiving it due to issues such as inadequate communication and denial of services. Regular exams for cancer and medical care for pregnant women were difficult to obtain for some of the same reasons. About 10 percent of immigrant detainees are women.

Amnesty International, another organization that monitors human rights abuses, reported that immigrants seeking asylum might spend as long as ten months in detention and some had even been behind bars for several years. ICE said that the average time in detention was only thirty-seven days. While the government spends about $95 per day on incarceration, release into the community costs as little as $12 per day.

Thousands of those being detained are undocumented immigrants who crossed the southwestern border of the United States. Those who have been caught by immigration officials are being detained until they can be brought into court. These first-time offenders have been told that they would be sent back across the border. But those who were caught returning were given stiffer sentences. As part of Operation Streamline, they can be incarcerated for up to six months. Many serve time at a facility in Laredo, Texas, operated by The GEO Group, Inc., a private prison company. Nearby is another facility run by Corrections Corporation of America.

Federal agents have picked up other undocumented immigrants in raids on employers of illegal immigrants. In 2008, ICE agents raided Agriprocessors, a meatpacking plant in Iowa, and arrested three hundred employees, charging them with being undocumented immigrants. Most were found guilty and sentenced to prisons in Florida and Louisiana.

At one of these facilities in Florida, 2,100 Haitians seeking asylum in the United States were held in detention. In 2006, the detainees reported that they were subject to "overcrowding, filth, beatings, [and] predatory phone prices" to use a pay phone to call family members. In addition, "[s]ome of the prisoners, who [had]

Guantánamo Bay

The United States' presence at Guantánamo Bay dates back to the late 1800s, when U.S. marines were killed there during the Spanish-American War. A few years later, the United States took possession of the 45-square-mile (117-square-kilometer) site on the southeastern end of Cuba and used it as a naval base. Over the years, Guantánamo has been involved in various controversies, though all of them have been overshadowed by the controversies that began in January 2002.

Shortly after the September 11, 2001, terrorist attacks on the United States, President George W. Bush decided to establish a camp at Guantánamo to detain suspected terrorists captured during the president's "war on terror" in Afghanistan, and later Iraq. The first such prisoners arrived at Guantánamo on January 11, 2002. A week later, the government determined that the detainees were terrorists, and therefore they were not entitled to the same liberties as other American prisoners—or even prisoners of war. Claims that the prisoners were treated inhumanely followed, bolstered by a photo showing the detainees handcuffed, shackled, and on their knees, with their ears, eyes, and mouths covered. Soon human rights organizations, and eventually the general public, spoke out against the perceived cruel treatment of the detainees. Allegations surfaced that the prisoners were subjected to sexual humiliation, sleep deprivation, a form of mock drowning called waterboarding, and other inhumane acts.

Cries began to surface to shut down the camp, and some prisoners were released. In 2008, the U.S. Supreme Court ruled that the remaining detainees at Guantánamo had the right to challenge their detention in federal court. In January 2009, President Barack Obama ordered the detention center at Guantánamo Bay to be closed within a year. As of early 2011, Obama's plan to transfer those held at Guantánamo Bay to U.S. prisons while they await trial was tied up in the political realm, with tough-on-terror Republicans opposing such transfers.

already signed their deportation documents, [were] still being held by ICE. . . . Some prisoners [were there] for years awaiting deportation. One [had] been [there] for over three years." As Mark Dow wrote in *Social Research Quarterly*, the immigration detention system is designed to punish those held behind bars.

Some politicians do not have a problem with the mistreatment of undocumented criminals. U.S. representative Brian Bilbray, a Republican from California, said, "If they really hate the detention facility, they can always say 'Forget it, I want to go home' (to their own country). But they see this as a great opportunity to leverage the system so they can stay here legally."

In 2010, the American Bar Association (ABA), America's leading professional association of lawyers, pointed out that judges who hear immigration cases are overwhelmed by the sheer number of them. As a result, those awaiting hearings often spend long periods in detention centers, at a substantial cost to taxpayers. The ABA called for a new court system devoted only to dealing with immigration cases, to speed up the trial process and cut down on detention.

American Jails reported that staff members in jails that house undocumented immigrants, many of whom do not speak English, need to be trained in speaking a foreign language—especially Spanish—so they can respond to emergencies. About two-thirds of immigrants in detention are in these jails.

The issue of Americans having to learn foreign languages to function in the United States rankles many people. Republican Tim James, who for a time was a candidate for Alabama governor in 2010, is one such person. Speaking about his state's practice of printing driver's license exams in twelve different languages, he said, "This is Alabama. We speak English. If you want to live here, learn it. We're only giving that test in English if I'm governor. . . . We welcome non-English speaking people, who are legally in the U.S., to Alabama. However, if you want to drive in our states,

Immigration raids often separate families when some family members are deported.

public safety concerns dictate that you need to speak English."

In 2009, President Barack Obama's administration vowed to improve conditions in the immigration detention system—at least that part run by the Bureau of Prisons and private contractors. Brian P. Hale, an official with ICE, explained that those conditions symbolized the past, and that in the future every death would be investigated and more attention given to detainee care.

Late in 2009, ICE issued new guidelines for immigration detention reform initiatives. These included a review of all facilities to ensure that they are making improvements. ICE also pledged to investigate those facilities run by private prison companies to make sure that they made reforms. More staff members would be hired at detention facilities to provide oversight of conditions and opera-

Undocumented Immigrants in Detention

Approximately 35,000 people, or one-fifth of all inmates in federal prisons, are undocumented immigrants. Approximately 270,000 inmates in local jails are undocumented immigrants—held there because there is no room for them in federal penitentiaries. Some of them are being held for entering the United States illegally, while others have also committed more serious crimes.

The Government Accountability Office compiled a report on these undocumented immigrants in local, state, and federal detention centers. The study focused on more than 55,000 undocumented immigrants who had crossed U.S. borders illegally. On average, each of them had been arrested eight times for criminal offenses. About 45 percent of these arrests were for drug offenses and illegal entry. Another 15 percent of the immigrants were arrested for small thefts, damaging property, or stealing automobiles. About 12 percent were arrested for offenses such as murder, assault, and sexual assault. Arizona, California, and Texas, those states nearest the southern border with Mexico, accounted for most of the arrests. In April 2010, Arizona enacted a controversial law that requires police to ask for immigration papers from anyone they suspect might be in the country illegally. The law also targets employers who hire illegal immigrants. The law was subjected to numerous legal challenges.

tions. In addition, ICE said its staff would evaluate all immigrants being detained to determine which ones could be released into the community under alternative programs—such as electronic monitoring. Not everyone was pleased when, in 2009, the Hutto facility released all families held in custody there and was transformed into a detention center for women only.

U.S. representative Lamar Smith, a Republican from Texas, was concerned by that and other reforms. While he said he was pleased that reforms were being made, he believes a suggested move to no longer detain entire families could lead to the releasing of "more illegal immigrants on the streets of American communities. The wealth of evidence proves that alternatives to detention and catch and release don't work. When illegal immigrants are not detained before deportation, they never return home."

Meanwhile, ICE must often carry on investigations that last many months to determine whether immigrants, such as those seeking asylum, are entitled to remain in the United States. To deal with the conditions under which immigrants are held during that time, Senator Joseph Lieberman, an Independent from Connecticut, has introduced the Secure and Safe Detention and Asylum Act. The bill was being debated in 2010. If passed, it would provide improved medical care to immigrant detainees, give aliens access to legal counsel to handle their cases, and create better conditions for families held in detention.

As of early 2011, several organizations—including the ACLU and the National Immigrant Justice Center—said that despite President Obama's vow to improve conditions in the immigration detention system, little had been accomplished.

8 Prison With and Without Parole

SERIAL KILLER GARY RIDGWAY IS CURRENTLY SERVING
a life sentence without parole for the murders of forty-eight women
in Washington State. Prosecutors agreed not to seek the death penalty when Ridgway offered to tell them where all the bodies of his
victims were buried. They also believed that life without parole for
Ridgway would safeguard society and prevent him from jeopardiz-
ing the lives of any other victims.

Dec. 3, 2003

Nov. 19, 2003

Nov. 19, 2003

Nov. 19, 2003

Gary Ridgway was sentenced to life without parole after pleading guilty to killing
forty-eight women over the course of about twenty years. Many don't think
that's a strong enough sentence.

Ridgway is one of more than 140,000 prisoners serving life sentences in the United States. Although Ridgway is white, about 66 percent of those serving life sentences are either African American or Hispanic. Generally, these life sentences are for murder, but they also may be for other crimes, such as rape or drug trafficking.

A life sentence does not always mean exactly what logic would indicate. In states such as Utah or California, a prisoner serving life may be considered for parole in less than ten years. In a state such as Colorado, parole will not be considered for forty to fifty years. However, in six states, including Illinois and Pennsylvania, all life sentences mean just that—there is no possibility of parole.

In those states that allow it, a prisoner can be granted parole only under certain circumstances. Generally, the prisoner's case is reviewed by a parole board, which listens to testimony about his or her behavior behind bars and determines whether he or she is deemed a threat to society. The way parole boards are selected has been criticized. As reported by the Sentencing Project, "[P]arole boards remain the domain of political appointees and two-thirds of states lack any standardized qualifications for service. This has resulted in a highly politicized process that too often discounts evidence and expert testimony." Some states, as a result, have eliminated parole boards. In those states, prisoners must simply serve out their sentence, with no hope of early release.

William Heirens, known as the Lipstick Killer because he wrote a message in lipstick on a wall at the scene of one of his murders, was sentenced to life in Illinois following his conviction for three murders in 1946. In time, he became the first person in Illinois to receive a four-year college degree while in prison. The elderly Heirens has diabetes and spends most of his time in a wheelchair. Though many might feel that Heriens poses little threat to society, his parole board stated in 2008 that he could not be released. "God will forgive you," a board member said, "but the state won't."

Betty Finn does not sympathize with Heirens either; he killed

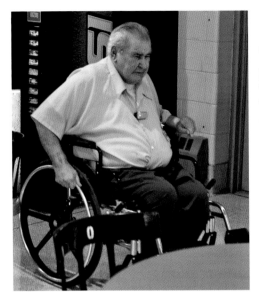

William Heirens has been in prison for sixty-five years for murdering three people. Though he is elderly and in a wheelchair, the state board turned down his plea for parole because of the severity of his crimes.

her six-year-old sister in 1946. "Can you imagine as a child to have this happen?" Finn said. "Can you imagine going to bed at night and all of a sudden your sister is not in her bed? . . . He was the bogeyman. I don't think you need to feel sorry for him. He chose his life and he chose his actions. . . . Keep him locked in jail."

Studies of people over the age of fifty who were released from prison after serving twenty-five years or more showed that relatively few of them ever committed another crime. In fact, the recidivism rate of such people in Ohio was zero, and in Pennsylvania it was only about 1.5 percent. This compares to an overall recidivism rate of roughly 67 percent for most prisoners released on parole. "Many lifers are kept in prison long after they represent a public safety threat," said Marc Maurer, executive director of the Sentencing Project.

On the other hand, some of those prisoners who are released do commit more crimes. Reginald McFadden was released from prison in Pennsylvania in 1994 after serving twenty-four years of a life sentence for murder. Soon afterward, he killed at least two more people and was returned to prison to serve a second life sentence. Regardless of how rare it may be, the impact a Reginald McFadden–type case has on the general public—and ultimately on the policies that govern parole cases and the politicians responsible for those policies—always is widespread.

In California, more than 30,000 inmates are serving life sentences. To obtain parole, their release must be approved by a parole board and then by the governor. In only a very few cases, however, has the governor approved a prisoner's release. A majority of Americans believe that state officials should be tough on criminals, especially those who have committed violent crimes, and should not permit them to return to society. However, others argue that if a prisoner has been rehabilitated—like some of those serving life sentences—he or she should be released.

Life Without Parole

Among those serving life sentences in the United States, about 41,000 have been given no opportunity for parole. Between 2003 and 2008, this population of prisoners has risen by 22 percent, thanks largely to new laws that have expanded the types of crimes that result in life sentences. The largest number of prisoners serving life without parole is incarcerated in California. Life without parole generally is reserved for prisoners who have committed murder, like Gary Ridgway. In most states, prisoners may serve either a life sentence or life without parole. The two terms can be confusing. "Life without parole" means exactly what it says: those who are given such sentences will spend the rest of their lives behind bars. However, "life sentences" often include indeterminate time frames, such as sentences of "twenty-five years to life." Other life sentences also are open to potential parole. The federal government has eliminated life sentences and have only life without parole for particularly violent crimes.

The number of these sentences has increased in response to political pressure placed on politicians for harsher sentencing. In addition, many people oppose the death penalty for moral, religious, financial, and other reasons. Due to the lengthy judicial process necessary to carry out the death penalty, killing a prisoner actually costs more than sentencing him or her to life in prison. People who oppose the death penalty often support a sentence of life without parole as an alternative. In those scenarios, the prisoner remains behind bars and society is protected.

In addition, such a sentence eliminates the chance that a prisoner who has been wrongfully accused of murder may be executed. The possibility of this injustice is another reason many people do not believe in the death penalty.

Prisoners on Parole

As of 2009, the United States had a total population of more than seven million people in the criminal justice system, or one in every thirty-one Americans. About 2.3 million were incarcerated, with the rest were either on probation or parole. Probation means that the person lives in the community but is being supervised by a probation officer. Many such people also have served time in jail. The population on parole numbers just over 800,000. Some experts argue that if probation had more services and could be strengthened, more offenders could be in the community than in prison or jail. The Pew Center on the States, a nonprofit research group, estimated that "for hundreds of thousands of lower-level inmates [drug users, for example], incarceration costs taxpayers far more than it saves in prevented crime."

The parole system was designed to help former inmates rehabilitate themselves. As an inmate prepares to be paroled, he or she may become part of a work-release program. This involves working at a job in the community during the day and returning to a correctional facility at night. Other prisoners are released to a halfway house, work at a job, but return to close supervision at the halfway house at night. Eventually, they are released to live on their own.

When prisoners are released from prison on parole, they become part of the caseload of a parole officer. The parole officer's responsibility is to monitor the parolee to ensure that he or she abides by the law. This means that the parolee does not commit another crime or violate the conditions of his or her parole, such as not showing up for periodic meetings with a parole officer. Many prisoners are habitual drug users, and one condition of parole is staying drug-free and alcohol-free. To monitor parolees, parole officers administer periodic drug tests. A parolee who fails a test may be returned to prison.

In addition, parole officers are expected to guide parolees into drug rehabilitation programs to help them deal with potential drug problems, help them find counseling for psychological problems, and direct them toward vocational training so they can find jobs. The intent is to keep the parolees from returning to prison, enable them to reform, and keep them in the community.

Unfortunately, these goals frequently aren't met. One reason is that the caseload for each parole officer has greatly increased, from about forty-five cases in the late twentieth century to more than seventy by the first decade of the twenty-first century. More money is being spent on building new prisons than on training and paying for more parole officers, which is an issue of contention for parole officers. One analysis in the *Journal of Offender Rehabilitation* reported that too few officers means that each officer has little time to focus on parolees as individuals and provide counseling or referrals to community agencies. Instead, officers "have little choice but to concentrate on surveillance . . . ," wrote Joel Caplan, a Ph.D. candidate at the University of Pennsylvania School of Social Policy & Practice. If a parolee violates parole, instead of finding him or her a counselor, a parole officer is more likely to send the person back to prison, simply because it is easier.

In testimony before the U.S. Congress in 2009, Stephen Manley, a superior court judge in California who deals with parole violations, said "Less than one-half . . . satisfy their conditions of parole supervision, including remaining abstinent from drugs or alcohol. Within 3 years of their release from prison, approximately two-thirds of inmates are charged with a new crime and over one-half are re-incarcerated either for a new crime or for a technical parole violation."

Judge Manley added that part of the problem is that parole officers often are unable to persuade parolees to comply with the conditions of their release. Most of these released prisoners are not strongly motivated to seek counseling or drug and alcohol rehabilitation. And in many cases other services—such as mental health counseling—are hard to find. "In my experience," Manley said, "most probation and parole officers direct offenders to find a place to live, get a job, report regularly, enter treatment, drug test, and stay out of trouble. The obligation is put nearly 100% on the offender and if he or she fails to follow directions, the answer is often more punishment."

These offenders often cannot easily access treatment, and therefore continue to use drugs. Estimates are that the system can treat only about 7 percent of the offenders, while more than 50 percent need treatment. Therefore, more people fail on parole and probation. One study by Dr. Faye Taxman at George Mason University found that most of the treatment is not very good and therefore people do not get much help anyway. The study found that the probation and parole system is not preventing reincarceration, and that expanding treatment services in the community would help tremendously.

To deal with this problem, many states have begun relying on drug courts. The concept originated in Florida in 1989 and has grown to about 2,500 programs nationwide. The drug court idea has shown that treatment can be more effective than just prison or jail. In this type of program, the court works with a parole officer and community rehabilitation services to monitor the parolee and provide counseling and treatment. The parolee is subject to regular drug testing, and if found in violation of parole, immediately is brought in front of the judge. The judge warns the parolee that continued violations can result in a return to prison. Studies in California and New York have shown that drug courts have significantly cut recidivism rates.

Parolees not only need help in the community, they also require programs while in prison to prepare them for release. A 2005 American Public Health Association study of young men and women released from correctional centers in New York City found that very few received any vocational training while they were incarcerated. Nevertheless, research showed that a parolee who had a job and was earning an income was less likely to be rearrested for committing a crime, such as selling drugs, to make money. In addition, the study revealed that the majority of women and young men did not attend drug rehabilitation programs offered in jail. (Budget cuts eventually brought an end to these programs.) The parolees also did not go to drug rehabilitation programs or vocational training programs after they were released, although these services were offered.

Budget cuts have impacted many programs designed to rehabilitate inmates. For example, the Deuel Vocational Institution in California has all but disappeared, leaving affected inmates with little job training. Jails also are lacking in rehabilitation programs. Amy Solomon, a senior research associate at the Urban Institute, a nonprofit organization in Washington, D.C., reported that almost 70 percent of inmates suffer from substance abuse and 60 percent lack high school diplomas or GEDs. She explained that they need programs that will help rehabilitate and educate them so they are less likely to return to jail. These programs will increase the likelihood that they will find a job—assuming there are enough jobs out there for them to find. Prisons also must work more closely with community organizations, such as treatment facilities and vocational training programs, to help inmates make a more successful transition back into the community.

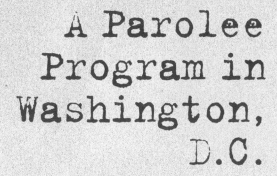

A Parolee Program in Washington, D.C.

Many parolees come out of prison with few, if any, resources. They may have no place to live and suffer from psychological illnesses as well as drug and alcohol addictions. With large caseloads, parole officers are often unable to monitor technical parole violations if parolees do not show up for drug treatment programs and continue using drugs. In addition, technical violations usually involve costly and time-consuming hearings. Parole officers with heavy caseloads may not have time to deal with these violations unless they get help.

To deal with this problem, the federal government has established the Court Services and Offender Supervision Agency for the District of Columbia. Parolees know that if they commit a violation, various punishments will be used to deal with them. Parolees may be monitored with electronic ankle bracelets, and they may be placed in the Re-Entry and Sanctions Center. This center, which has room for over one hundred residents, provides a twenty-eight-day program of counseling. It is aimed at inmates who have just been released from prison and have a high risk of returning for additional offenses. After this program, most parolees are immediately referred to a drug treatment facility for continued counseling. The agency has also instituted a 180-day treatment program in a facility for up to thirty-two offenders who have returned to drug abuse or who have been guilty of another technical violation of their parole. Finally, the agency runs the Vocational Opportunities for Training, Education and Employment program to help parolees train for jobs in areas such as food services and construction. This is another way of helping parolees avoid being sent back to prison.

9 Compassion or Punishment?

SUSAN ATKINS CONFESSED TO HER MOST notorious crime. In 1969, she said, she held down pregnant actress Sharon Tate and stabbed her sixteen times in Tate's home in Los Angeles. Before leaving the crime scene, Atkins used Tate's blood to write the word "PIG" on the front door. In 1993, Atkins described Tate's last words. "She asked me to let the baby live," Atkins said. "I told her I didn't have mercy for her." At her trial years earlier, Atkins said, "[I have] no guilt for what I've done. It was right then and I still believe it was right."

Atkins, who committed the crime as part of Charles Manson's "family" of followers, eventually was convicted of the murder of Tate and seven others. She was sent to prison to serve a life sentence. Over the years, Atkins received thirteen parole hearings, and was denied her freedom at each of them, despite claims that she was remorseful, and had become a Christian, as well as reports from staff that she had been a near-perfect prisoner.

Because of the brutality of her crimes, no one ever believed Atkins had a chance to get out of prison. But, prior to her thirteenth attempt at parole in September 2009, some people's opinions had changed. There were those who believed Atkins should be released and actually might have a chance to be, because she was terminally ill with brain cancer and unlikely to live much longer. Her family argued that she should be allowed to die at home, and that the state would save $10,000 a day in medical costs if they released her. Her

Susan Atkins died in prison, riddled with cancer, almost forty years after her conviction for her role in the murder of Sharon Tate.

husband, whom she had married while she was in prison, said, "She's paralyzed [over] just about 85 percent of her body. She can nod her head and she can look left and right and she has limited use of her left arm." Even Vincent Bugliosi, the prosecutor who had helped convict Atkins four decades earlier, believed she should be released. He said, "She's already paid substantially for her crime, close to 40 years behind bars. She has terminal cancer. The mercy she [is] asking for is so minuscule. She's about to die. It's not like we're going to see her down at Disneyland."

Even after watching Atkins wheeled into the parole hearing in a hospital bed, Tate's family did not budge from the stance they had held the previous four decades—that Atkins should die in prison for what she did to their relative. Sharon Tate's younger sister, Debra Tate, told the parole board she "will pray for (Atkins's) soul when she draws her last breath, but until then I think she should remain in this controlled situation." Steve Chapman, a noted syndicated columnist for the *Chicago Tribune*, chimed in on the case. He said, "[M]aybe there is money to be saved by letting . . . Atkins out of their taxpayer-financed housing. But few government funds were ever better spent. And it's hard to see why people who have committed violent crimes deserve any consideration beyond the fair trial and sentencing they have already gotten. Compassionate release is compassionate only to criminals, not their victims."

In Atkins's case the compassion approach did not work, possibly due in part to the high-profile status and horrific nature of her crimes. She was again denied parole, and died less than a month later. But there are instances where prisoners in the United States have been released under special circumstances. In fact, the Federal Bureau of Prisons has a policy relating to that very issue. It is called compassionate release, and allows an inmate the right to appeal to his or her warden for release during "particularly extraordinary or compelling circumstances which could not reasonably have been foreseen by the court at the time of sentencing." Such a request must be fairly specific, and several officials must approve it before the release can be granted. In recent years, thanks partially to a poor economy and a surging prison population, support for utilizing compassionate release laws has grown within the correctional system. However, actual release numbers have not grown accordingly. In 2009 in California, just three prisoners were granted compassionate release. The same year in Alabama, where prisons were overflowing, four persons were granted release.

Sometimes, however, the compassionate release appeal does work. Suffering from cancer, Cinderella Marrett was granted such a release in New York in 2009. Just two years earlier, Marrett, then in her early seventies, had been caught smuggling cocaine in her girdle at a New York airport. During Marrett's parole hearing, her daughter argued that Marrett only had the cocaine to help offset the cost of her medical expenses. Once granted parole, Marrett was released to a nursing home. She died early the next year.

Fighting for Victims' Rights

There are groups formed specifically to speak for victims when they cannot, or even when they can, do it for themselves. Over the years, victims' rights has become a controversial subject, and the federal government has enacted several laws that guarantee rights to victims of crime. In 1975, a nonprofit group, the National Organization for Victim Assistance, was founded to promote the rights of crime victims across the United States. Today, every state has a similar type of group. These groups often advocate for the victims of crime in many settings, including in the legislature, in the courtroom, and at parole hearings. Many groups even provide financial support for victims.

Miriam Shehane is one such victims' advocate. She became involved in victims' rights, as many other people have done, after suffering a personal tragedy. In 1976, Shehane's twenty-one-year-old daughter was abducted from a convenience store parking lot in

Alabama, then raped and murdered. Shehane subsequently began the victims' rights movement in Alabama by forming Victims of Crime and Leniency, in 1982, as a way of helping her deal with the pain of her loss. In her view, criminals give up their rights to any compassion the moment they are convicted of their crimes. "I would like to know that the two serving time in prison for killing my daughter have to think they're not in a place that is a place to reside with the comforts of home," she told author Sasha Abramsky in 2005. "Are they able to touch [visitors]? I would hope not. I would like to know they had to pay for their housing. They should have to grow their own food." Shehane went on to say that she believed more people, killers and rapists included, should be executed for their crimes, and that "[i]t should be a shameful thing to be incarcerated—and it's not anymore."

Ted Deeds of the Law Enforcement Alliance of America, a strong advocate for the rights of victims, agreed that prison should not be easy and the goal is to punish criminals. He said, "Prisons have become mini-resorts and it's disgusting, and it's particularly disgusting to crime victims. We strongly believe that prison is meant to be punishment, a deterrent and a prevention tool, not a resort experience."

The Role of Money

Finances play a large role in the debate over who should be locked up and for how long. It is expensive to keep someone behind bars, especially those who are on their death beds and require special medical attention. Releasing them from prison, compassion advocates say, would change who pays for the medical treatment. In Shehane's home state of Alabama, for example, it costs roughly $65,000 per year to treat terminally ill or infirm inmates on average. That money comes from the prison system. Allowing such inmates to be released would shift the cost of their care to the federally funded Medicare program, or the state-funded and federally funded Medicaid program. Victims' rights advocates say that, in the end, taxpayers still pay for the cost, so no money is really saved by releasing terminally ill inmates, and they should stay behind bars.

The issue of whether or not inmates deserve compassion is not topical only when the prisoner is critically ill and has petitioned for a compassionate release. There are people who believe prison is a punishment, and that those serving time do not deserve much consideration at all. After all, they argue, no compassion was shown for the victims, so why should there be any shown to the perpetrators? Offering prisoners educational, counseling, and job-training opportunities does not amount to a punishment. That amounts to compassion, and criminals do not deserve any.

Politics also play a large role in what happens inside prison walls. Most politicians will not openly advocate for punishing criminals, because being perceived as not caring for fellow human beings would be damaging to their careers. Instead, politicians indirectly increase the punishment prisoners receive while behind bars by voting to slash prison budgets. This has happened many times over the past few years, due to the country's extended economic downturn. Republican victories during the midterm elections of 2010 helped swing the country toward a more tough-on-crime stance. Newly elected officials in several states have proposed major cuts to prison budgets. In Florida, governor Rick Scott proposed cutting the state's $2.5 billion prison budget by $1 billion a year. Proponents of the proposal find benefits in the savings. Opponents picture their streets full of recently released criminals.

Exactly where the general public stands on compassion versus punishment for prisoners is not easy to determine. In September 2010, three national research groups joined together to attempt to figure it out by conducting a comprehensive phone survey on the subject of crime and punishment. The results were enlightening. According to the survey, voters believed that:

- 22 percent of prisoners could be released from prison without threatening public safety;
- Cuts to prison spending would be far more desirable than cuts to education spending, health care spending, or raising property or business taxes;
- Access to treatment and job-training programs needs to be readily available to prisoners in order for them to be productive members of society when they are released;
- There are too many low-risk, nonviolent offenders in prison, and better, cost-effective alternatives to incarceration are needed for such criminals.

As far as what the "primary purpose of prisons" should be, the survey's results were inconclusive. Thirty-one percent of respondents said it should be to protect society, 25 percent said it should be to rehabilitate people, and 20 percent said it should be to punish offenders. Such diversity is common, and is another reason why determining how offenders should be treated is and always has been such a controversial issue.

10 Prisons—The Next Decade

VIOLENT CRIME RATES IN THE UNITED STATES ARE AT their lowest levels in more than a decade, as reported by the Bureau of Justice, an agency that compiles these statistics for the federal government. This certainly seems to be good news. But when it is pointed out that much of the decline is due to stiff sentencing and lengthy prison terms, resulting in criminals being taken off the streets and placed in overcrowded prisons, which have their own problems, the good news seems a bit less so.

In the state of Louisiana, which has the highest rate of impris-

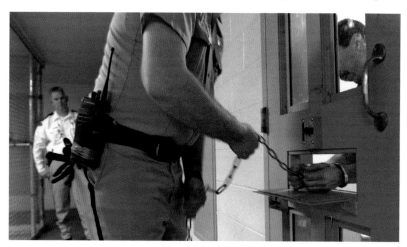

The murder of a guard by prisoners at this private facility in New Mexico was a wake-up call for the state to take a look at the serious problems within the correctional system. John Beard, chief of security at the facility, watches from a distance as an inmate is handcuffed before being taken out of his cell.

onment in the world, there are constant reports that mentally ill prisoners are mistreated, that prison guards use violence toward prisoners, and that those who are ill are prevented from receiving their medicine or seeing vision doctors.

Outside Los Angeles, in Lancaster prison, prisoners swelter in 100°F (38°C) heat during the summer because air-conditioning systems do not work. A center for temporarily housing inmates and processing their admittance to other facilities was designed to hold 2,200 prisoners but now holds 4,500. Gymnasiums have been outfitted with rows and rows of bunk beds to hold prisoners who cannot be put anywhere else because of overcrowding. At another California prison, Pelican Bay, a federal judge ruled that conditions were so bad that they could not "be squared with evolving standards of humanity or decency," and he ordered immediate reforms.

In Alabama, the state Department of Corrections also is trying to deal with "gross overcrowding" at its existing prisons, some of which are more than fifty years old. The state is under a court order to cut down on the number of prisoners at each facility. Instead of using publicly built prisons, however, Alabama is considering using privately run correctional facilities. Currently, Alabama has dealt with overcrowding by sending some of its prisoners to private facilities out of state, but this has cost over $12 million since 2002.

However, a state task force recommended building private facilities in Alabama for a variety of reasons. Costs of running the facility in Alabama would be about 10 to 15 percent less than in a state-run facility. The quality of care would be similar because both privately run and state-run correctional facilities provide the same variety of programs for inmates—including drug rehabilitation and vocational training. Training for prison staff is equivalent in each type of facility. In addition, the private companies could build facilities faster than the state, and at lower cost. This would enable Alabama to comply more rapidly with the court order to reduce overcrowding.

Meanwhile, other states have begun looking at a different set of options to improve prison conditions. With costs rising and budgets tight, these states have reasoned that more prisons may not be the best solution to their problems. For decades, Texas has been one of the states with the highest rates of incarceration. However, the costs of keeping so many people in prison have become more than the state budget can tolerate. So, in 2007, a group of politicians began what was dubbed a "reinvestment movement," during which plans for building three new prisons were abandoned and the state began spending more money on drug abuse programs and mental health counseling for prisoners and parolees. In addition, caseloads for parole officers were capped so they could spend more time with each parolee. As a result, the number of parolees violating parole and returning to prison dropped by 25 percent. By 2008, the rate of increase in the prison population had declined to 0.4 percent from 3 percent eight years earlier. Indeed, Texas now has one of the highest rates of decline in people being incarcerated.

In 2008, New Mexico governor Bill Richardson's prison task force recommended a variety of strategies to cut down on the number of people being sent to prison and those who were returning for parole violations. The recidivism rate in New Mexico is about 47 percent, which is below the national average, but still high. The cost to the taxpayers is about $31,000 per prisoner per year. A majority of the people being sentenced to prison or returning to prison have substance abuse problems. Therefore, the task force has recommended the expansion of drug courts and other treatment programs.

For those reentering the community, the New Mexico Task Force recommended that mentors be assigned to prisoners being released from prison to help guide them during their reentry into the community. In addition, the task force recommended that halfway houses be expanded to house more parolees in supervised environments within the community. Also, program models are being

Jimmy Parker has been sorting recyclables at a Chicago waste management plant for six months as part of a program to provide jobs for former prisoners.

recommended to help parolees and their families work together to ensure the success of each prisoner's reentry.

In recent years, the state of New York has initiated similar programs that have increased vocational education for inmates so they would be better prepared to find jobs. Prisons have also improved medical care and mental health services, while the state has provided more community programs to help parolees. The recidivism rate in New York is about 33 percent, well below the national average.

Georgia has faced a rising inmate population that has required state political leaders to devise alternatives to prison. In the early 2000s, these programs have been initiated by Georgia commissioner of corrections James Donald. Among them is the use of an assessment tool called Correctional Offender Management Profiling for Alternative Sanctions (COMPAS). This enables law enforcement officials to determine if people convicted of a crime are at risk of committing further violence, failing to report to probation officers if they are placed on probation, and recidivism if they are paroled. It also indicates their need for various types of treatment programs.

A Restitution
Program

In her book, *Dreams from the Monster Factory: A Tale of Prison, Redemption and One Woman's Fight to Restore Justice to All,* Sunny Schwartz wrote about an innovative prison program that she initiated in California during the 1990s. Her program, Resolve to Stop the Violence Project (RSVP), has reduced recidivism during the two decades that it has operated. In group therapy sessions, prisoners are urged to confront the ways in which they have hurt other people—family, friends, victims—by their behavior. The program helps prisoners recognize what they have done, take responsibility for their actions, and even admit to family and friends the harm that they may have caused them. Don, a bank robber, recognized that he had a drug problem but refused to confront his own violent behavior. The RSVP program helped him recognize and deal with his anger and violence. Among those who participated in the sixteen-week program, recidivism was 82 percent less than among those who did not participate. The program still is being used by the San Francisco Sheriff's Department.

This type of instrument allows officials to decide whether a criminal should be incarcerated or placed on probation. Further, if the criminal is incarcerated, it enables corrections officials to help plan a program of treatment and education that will be most beneficial for the prisoner. Finally, when parole is considered, the assessment tool helps corrections officers plan a treatment program in the community for the inmate that has the potential to reduce the likelihood of his or her return to prison. However, as of 2010, the COMPAS test was not being widely used in Georgia's prisons. There are other inmate assessment tools used in prisons, as well.

Georgia has expanded available housing for parolees in the community. In the past, some inmates who had been granted parole were forced to remain in prison because adequate housing was unavailable. By increasing the amount of housing available for parolees, and releasing them from prison, the state saved millions of dollars. Another Georgia program has lined up businesses to hire parolees as employees. Studies have shown that for a parolee, having a job as well as adequate housing are among the most effective ways to reduce recidivism.

Exactly what the future holds for the American prison system specifically, and the nation's criminal justice system in general, is uncertain. Will tough-on-crime laws lead to even more criminals being sent to prison—and will new prisons be built to accommodate such offenders? Or will the populations of current facilities continue to swell until a tragic event, such as the deadly riots at Attica, New York, and the New Mexico State Penitentiary, forces policy changes? Will new ideas such as in-home monitoring and community supervision programs, or yet-to-be-created lighter crime laws relieve the overcrowding? Moreover, will society as a whole revert toward a trend of compassion, or will the belief that those who break laws should be punished continue to rule the day? Whatever happens, one thing is certain: there will most certainly be heated debate before each change occurs.

Timeline

1790	Walnut Street Jail opens in Philadelphia; marks beginning of Pennsylvania system
1821	Prison opens in Auburn, New York; marks beginning of Auburn system
1870	National Prison Association founded
1876	Elmira Reformatory for youths opens in New York
1895	First federal penitentiary opens at Fort Leavenworth, Kansas
1899	Juvenile court system begins in Chicago
1919	Prohibition begins
1929	Hawes-Cooper Act passed, restricting transportation of prison-made items
1933	Prohibition repealed
1971	War on drugs begins; riot at Attica Correctional Facility, New York
1982	Forty-two states ordered by federal courts to improve prison conditions
2002	U.S. detention center opens at Guantánamo Bay, Cuba
2003	Congress passes Prison Rape Elimination Act
2007	Congress passes Second Chance Act
2010	U.S. Supreme court bans sentences of life in prison without parole for juveniles, except in cases of murder

Notes

Chapter 1

p. 9, "The jail was . . . ": W. Storrs Lee, "Stone Walls Do Not a Prison Make," *American Heritage*, 2 (February 1967), www.americanheritage.com/articles/magazine/ah/1967/2/1967_2_40.shtml (accessed July 21, 2010).

p. 9, "As reported by writer W. Storrs Lee . . . ": *The American Prison* (New York: The American Correctional Association, 1983),14–16.

p. 10, "An alternative to the Pennsylvania . . . ": *The American Prison*, 28–51.

p. 10, "Under the 'Auburn' system . . . ": *The American Prison*, 48–50.

p. 11, "Instead of being punished . . . ": *The American Prison*, 88.

p. 12, "Humane treatment . . . ": *The American Prison*, 91.

p. 12, "During the last quarter . . . ": *The American Prison*, 93.

p. 15, "Over the next four decades . . . ": *The American Prison*, 78.

p. 16, "Regardless, beginning in Chicago . . . ": "Prison Reforms in American History," http://history.sandiego.edu/gen/soc/prison.html (accessed November 25, 2009).

p. 17, "Though reform was . . . ": *The American Prison*, 130–137.

p. 17, "total control . . . ": *The American Prison*, 137.

p. 17 "Stephen Cox, author of the . . . ": Stephen Cox, *The Big House* (New Haven, CT: Yale University Press, 2009), 58.

p. 17, "Meanwhile, the federal government . . . ": "Prison Reforms in American History."

p. 19, "While the prison population was . . . ": "Prisons: History—Modern Prisons," http://law.jrank.org/pages/1782/Prisons-History-Modern-prisons.html (accessed November 25, 2009).

p. 19, "The offender was perceived . . . ": *The American Prison*, 193.

p. 19, "It was at this point . . . ": *The American Prison*, 148.

p. 20, "By the mid-1970s . . . ": *The American Prison*, 215.

p. 21, "One former prison aide . . . ": Roger Morris, *The Devil's Butcher Shop: The New Mexico Prison Uprising* (Albuquerque: University of New Mexico Press, 1983), 143.

p. 23, "Deliberate indifference by prison personnel . . . ": Cornell University Law School, *Estelle* v. *Gamble*, www4.law.cornell.edu/supct/html/historics/USSC_CR_0429_0097_ZS.html (accessed November 26, 2009).

p. 238, "The Constitution does not . . . ": *The American Prison*, 221.

Chapter 2

p. 26, "a sign of success for them . . . ": Jill Furness, "Fighting for the Futures of Young Offenders," *Corrections Today* 3 (June 2009).

p. 27, "We have 5 percent . . . ": "Webb's Prison Crusade," *Nation*, May 4, 2009, 4–5.

p. 28, "Noted criminologist Charles H. Logan . . . ": *Criminal Justice: Opposing Viewpoints* (San Diego,: Greenhaven, 1998), 29.

p. 28, "In 1918, for example . . . ": *The American Prison* (New York: The American Correctional Association, 1983), 191.

p. 28, "By the first decade . . . ": David Cole, "Can Our Shameful Prisons Be Reformed?" *New York Review of Books*, November 19, 2009, 41.

p. 28, "By way of comparison . . . ": Nigel Holmes, "Lock Up, U.S.A.," *American History*, October 2009, 26.

p. 29, "One of every eleven . . . ": Alton Maddox Jr., "No Stimulus Plan for Black Inmates," *New York Amsterdam News*, March 12, 2009, 12.

p. 29, "Women are the fastest growing . . . ": Amy Fettig, "Women Prisoners: Altering the Cycle of Abuse," *Human Rights* 2 (Spring 2009).

p. 29, "In fact, states . . . ": Holmes, "Lock Up, U.S.A."

p. 30, "The problem is especially bad . . . ": Solomon Moore, "California State Assembly Approves Prison Population," *New York Times*, September 1, 2009.

p. 30, "For the past few years . . . ": Moore, "California State Assembly Approves Prison Population."

p. 30, "As reported by the National . . . ": Solomon Moore, "Study of Rape in Prisons Counts 60,500 Attacks," *New York Times*, June 23, 2009.

p. 32, "In addition, many states . . . ": Solomon Moore, "Mentally Ill Offenders Stretch the Limits of Juvenile Justice," *New York Times*, August 10, 2009.

p. 32, "While tougher sentencing laws . . . ": "Prisons are Expensive," *State Prisons* (June 2009).

p. 32, "In California in 2009 . . . ": Michael Farrell, "Parole Holds Key to California Prison Overcrowding," *Christian Science Monitor*, September 27, 2009.

p. 33, "This is all aimed . . . ": Senate Judiciary Committee, Reducing Recidivism at the Local Level, congressional testimony of Amy Solomon, November 5, 2009.

p. 33, "Dan Lungren, the former . . . ": Daniel E. Lungren, "Victims and The Exclusionary Rule," *Harvard Journal of Law and Public Policy* (Spring 1996): 695–701.

Chapter 3

p. 34, "During the early 1980s . . . ": Jens Soering, "Life Without Parole," *Christian Century*, August 12, 2008, 28–31.

p. 34, "About ten years later . . . ": Solomon Moore, "Study Finds Record Number of Inmates Serving Life," *New York Times*, July 23, 2009.

p. 35, "One specific example . . . ": Maureen Cavanaugh and Pat Finn, "Prison Crisis: Overcrowded and Unconstitutional," KPBS, October 5, 2009, www.kpbs.org/news/2009/oct/05/prison-crisis-overcrowded-and-unconstitutional (accessed January 26, 2010).

p. 35, "In reaction to . . . ": Bureau of Justice Statistics, "Drug Law Violations: Enforcement," Drugs and Crime Facts, www.ojp.usdoj.gov/bjs/def/enforce.htm (accessed December 12, 2008).

p. 35, "As reported in 2009 . . . ": Alex Coolman, "Addressing Drug Policing and Racial Disparities: An Interview with Ryan King of the Sentencing Project," Drug Law Blog, July 16, 2008, http://druglaw.typepad.com/drug_law_blog/2008/07/addressing-drug.html (accessed December 12, 2008).

p. 37, "He wrote that . . . ": Alton Maddox, "No Stimulus Plan for Black Inmates," *New York Amsterdam News*, March 12, 2009.

p. 37, "Prison populations . . . ": Moore, "Study Finds Record Number of Inmates Serving Life."

p. 38, "As executive director . . . ": R. David LaCourse Jr., "Three Strikes in Review," Washington Policy Center, 1997.

p. 38, "[J]udges have little . . . ": Amy Fettig, "Women Prisoners: Altering the Cycle of Abuse," *Human Rights: Journal of the Section of Individual Rights & Responsibilities* (Spring 2009).

p. 39, "And five states . . . " J. J. Hermes, "5 States Spend More on Prisons Than on Colleges," *Chronicle of Higher Education*, March 14, 2008.

p. 39, "As a result, these states . . . ": *The World Almanac and Book of Facts*, 2009 (Strongsville, OH: World Almanac, 2008), 473.

p. 40, "Housing prison populations . . . ": "Prisons Are Expensive," State Legislatures (June 2009): 6.

p. 40, "California passed legislation . . . ": Solomon Moore, "California State Assembly Approves Prison Legislation," *New York Times*, September 1, 2009.

p. 40, "In 1975 . . . ": David Cole, "Can Our Shameful Prisons Be Reformed?" *New York Review of Books*, November 19, 2009.

p. 40, "As a result . . . ": Lexington, "A Nation of Jailbirds," *Economist*, April 4, 2009, 40.

p. 41, "In August 2009 . . . ": CBS, "Chino Inmate Riot Blamed on Overcrowding," August 11, 2009. http://cbs2.com/local/Chino.Prison.Inmates.2.1124095.html (accessed December 9, 2009).

p. 41, "California's prisons spokesperson said . . . ": CBS, "Chino Inmate Riot Blamed on Overcrowding."

p. 42, "The reasons for incarcerations . . . ": Howard Snyder and Jeanne Stinchcomb, "Do Higher Incarceration Rates Mean Lower Crime Rates?" *Corrections Today* (October 2006).

p. 42, "One study published in 2006 . . . ": R. Liedka, A. Piehl, and B. Useem. " The Crime-Control Effect of Incarceration: Does Scale Matter?" *Criminology and Public Policy* (May 2006): 245–276.

p. 42, "Due to the economic recession . . . ,": Kenneth Hartman, "The Recession Behind Bars," *New York Times*, September 6, 2009.

p. 43, "Former Republican congressman . . . ": Iver Peterson, "Cutting Down on Amenities to Achieve No-Frills Jails, *New York Times*, July 10, 1995. www.nytimes.com/1995/07/10/nyregion/cutting-down-on-amenities-to-achieve-no-frills-jails.html?pagewanted=2 (accessed December 18, 2010).

p. 43, "The recession has led . . . ": Jennifer Steinhauer, "Arizona May Put All State Prisons in Private Hands," *New York Times*, October 24, 2009.

p. 44, "Overcrowding in Jails": "Bail Burden Keeps U.S. Jails Stuffed with Inmates," NPR, January 22, 2010, http://forums.somethingawful.com/showthrea.php?threadid=3257588 (accessed January 22, 2010).

p. 45, "However, a study . . . ": "What to Do About the Prison Problem: The Pros and Cons of Privatized Prisons in Alabama."

p. 45, "In addition . . . ": Gaes, "Cost, Performance Studies Look at Prison Privatization."

Chapter 4

p. 47, "When a criminal is sentenced . . . ": Patricia Hardyman et al., "Prisoner Intake Systems," U.S. Department of Justice, National Institute of Corrections, 2004, v11–20.

p. 48, "To put it bluntly . . . ": Clyde Hoffman, "California Blasted for Poor Prison Health Care," All Things Considered, NPR, October 14, 2004, www.npr.org/templates/story/story.php?storyId=4109523 (accessed December 21, 2009).

p. 49, "Henderson based his decision . . . ": Joe Domanick, "Anatomy of a Prison," *Los Angeles Magazine*, September 4, 2009.

p. 49, "Results of a nationwide survey . . . ": Andrew Wilper et al., "The Health and Health Care of US Prisoners: Results of a Nationwide Survey," *American Journal of Public Health* (April 2009).

p. 50, "In 2004, Crowley wrote . . . ": Michael Crowley, "Outrageous! Crime Pays . . . If You Need Top-Notch Medical Care," www.rd.com/your-america-inspiring-people-and-stories/thats-outrageous----prisoners-rights-to-free-medical-care/article27400.html (accessed July 14, 2010).

p. 51, "The challenge for prison health . . . ": Gary Maynard, "Correctional Health Continues to Provide Quality Care," *Corrections Today* (October 2007).

p. 51, "That fact does not bother . . . ": Crowley, "Outrageous!"

p. 51, "Correctional health care is on . . . ": Maynard, "Correctional Health Continues to Provide Quality Care."

p. 52, "Indeed, about one-half . . . ": Kim Krisberg, "Serious Mental Health Problems Prevalent Among U.S. Inmates," The Nation's Health (November 2006).

p. 52, "The number of mentally ill prisoners . . . ": Jeffrey Ferro, *Prisons* (New York: Facts on File, 2006), 54.

p. 52, "A study of women . . . ": Jeff Blum, "Identifying and Treating Mental Illness: One Jail System's Story," *Corrections Today* (August 2007).

p. 54, "The number of AIDS . . . ": Ronald Braithwaite and Kimberly Arriola, "Male Prisoners and HIV Prevention: A Call for Action Ignored," *American Journal of Public Health* (September 2008).

p. 55, "George Sanges . . . ": Stephanie Chen, "Prison Health-Care Costs Rise as Inmates Grow Older and Sicker," CNN.Com2008, http://articles.cnn.com/2009-11-13/justice/aging.inmates_1_prison-inmate-largest-prison-systems-medical-costs?_s=PM:CRIME (accessed December 21, 2009).

p. 56, "Six states have . . . ": Anthony Sterns et al., "The Growing Wave of Older Prisoners: A National Survey of Older Prisoner Health, Mental Health and Programming," *Corrections Today* (August 2008).

p. 57, "Foremost among them are . . . ": Dana DiFilippo, "Growing Old Behind Bars," Philadelphia *Daily News*, May 8, 2006, A-3.

p. 57, "it was enough to sustain . . . ": Marlene Martin, "What Happened to Prison Education Programs?" SocialistWorker.org, June 2, 2009, http://socialistworker.org/2009/06/02/what-happened-to-prison-education (accessed December 12, 2009).

p. 58, "In one study . . . ": Gwendolyn Cuizon, "Education in Prison," Educational Issues, February 13, 2009, http://educationalissues.suite101.com/article.cfm/education_in_prison (accessed December 18, 2009).

p. 58, "Those who participate . . . ": "Higher Education Behind Bars: Postsecondary Prison Education Programs Make a Difference," American Council on Education, October 14, 2008.

p. 58, "According to another study . . . ": Gerald Gaes, "The Impact of Prison Education Programs on Post-Release Outcomes," Reentry Roundtable on Education, February 18, 2008.

p. 59, "We discovered . . . ": "Higher Education Behind Bars."

p. 59, "Cindie Fonesca . . . ": "State Prison-Education Programs Lose $250M . . . ,": KABC, December 4, 2009, http://abclocal.go.com/kabc/story?section=news/state&id=7160474&pt=print (accessed December 18, 2009).

p. 59, "In fact, a 2010 survey . . . ": "Cut Prison Spending, Spare Schools, Worried Californians Say," Public Policy Institute of California, January 2010, http://www.ppic.org/main/pressrelease.asp?p=990 (accessed on December 19, 2010).

Chapter 5

p. 60, "We have a policy of . . . ": Al Barker, "Homicides Reach Record Low Rate in New York City," *New York Times*, December 29, 2009.

p. 60, "Politicians boast that . . . ": Norman Seabrook, "Prison Violence on the Rise," *USA Today*, September 2005, http://findarticles.com/p/articles/mi_m1272/is_2724_134/ai_n15380394/ (accessed December 18, 2009).

p. 60, "It is likely that . . . ": Seabrook, "Prison Violence on the Rise."

p. 61, "Sasha Abramsky, an author . . . ": Sasha Abramsky, *American Furies: Crime, Punishment, and Vengeance in the Age of Mass Imprisonment* (Boston: Beacon Press, 2007), 170–177.

p. 62, "A Bureau of Justice Statistics . . . ": Pat Kaufman, "Prison Rape: Research Explores Prevalence, Prevention," NIJ Journal, March 2008.

p. 62, "Since that time . . . ": Janine M. Zweig and John Blackmore, "Strategies to Prevent Prison Rape," NIJ Journal (October 2008): 1–10.

p. 62, "Nevertheless, a 2006 study . . . ": Kaufman, "Prison Rape: Research Explores Prevalence, Prevention."

p. 63, "In the 2009 . . . ": U.S. Department of Justice, National Prison Rape Elimination Commission Report, 2009, 1–30.

p. 64, "Violence or the potential for violence . . . ": Marianne McNabb, "Translating Research into Practice: Improving Safety in Women's Facilities," U.S. Department of Justice, December 2008, 1–7.

p. 65, "In 1995, the Department of . . . ": Paul J. Biermann, "Improving Correctional Officer Safety: Reducing Inmate Weapons," *Corrections Today* (February 2006): 68.

p. 65, "In the pod . . . ": Commission on Safety and Abuse in America's Prisons, "Corrections Officers Describe a Difficult, Stressful Job and Conditions That Put Staff and Prisoners at Risk," 2005, www.prison commission.org/pres_release_110105.asp, (accessed December 18, 2009).

p. 66, "An obvious problem . . . ": Christine Tartaro and Marissa Levy, "Crowding, Violence and Direct Supervision Jails," *American Jails* (September/October 2008): 12–22; Christine Tartaro, "Are They Really Direct Supervision Jails?" *American Jails* (November/December 2006): 9–16.

pp. 66–67, "Direct Supervision Correctional Facilities": Interview by author.

p. 68, "Today's correctional officer . . . ": Commission on Safety and Abuse, "Corrections Officers Describe a Difficult, Stressful Job."

p. 69, "Officers later testified . . . ": New Jersey State Legislature, New Jersey Assembly Prison Gang Violence Task Force Final Report, 2006, 1–12.

p. 69, "In some prisons . . . ": William J. Morgan, "Correctional Officer Stress: A Review of the Literature, 1977–2007," *American Jails* (May/June 2009): 33–43.

p. 69, "Attacks on property or persons . . . ": Morgan, "Correctional Officer Stress: A Review of Literature, 1977–2007."

p. 70, "On June 20, 2008 . . . ": House Appropriations Subcommittee on Commerce, Justice, and Science, Challenges Facing Federal Prisons, congressional testimony of Bryan Lowry, March 10, 2009.

p. 71, "By no means are inmates . . . .": Will Bigham, "Conviction of Inmate Abuse Reinstated for Calif. Officer," *Inland Valley Daily Bulletin*, June 8, 2010, www.correctionsone.com/arrests-and-sentencing/articles/2079934-Conviction-of-inmate-abuse-reinstated-for-Calif-officer/ (accessed July 29, 2010).

Chapter 6

p. 72, "In 2008, Colton Harris-Moore," Kim Murphy, "Teen Fugitive Captures Imagination of Many," *Los Angeles Times*, November 8, 2009. http://articles.latimes.com/2009/nov/08/nation/na-fugitive-boy8 (accessed January 2, 2010).

p. 72, "The Harris-Moore case . . . ": U.S. Department of Justice, Census of Juveniles in Residential Placement Databook, Office of Juvenile Justice and Delinquency Prevention, 2006.

p. 73, "Although they make up a . . .": Howard Snyder and Melissa Sickmund, Statistical Briefing Book, Juveniles in Corrections: Custody Data, 2006, Office of Juvenile Justice and Delinquency Prevention, www.ojjdp. ncjrs.gov/ojstatbb/corrections/qa08203.asp?qaDate=2006 (accessed December 31, 2009).

p. 73, "One prepared in 2009 . . . ": Jeff Armour and Sarah Hammond, Minority Youth in the Juvenile Justice System: Disproportionate Minority Contact, National Conference of State Legislatures, January 2009, www.ncsl.org/print/cj/minoritiesinjj.pdf (accessed July 30, 2010).

p. 74, "Nationally . . . ": U.S. Department of Justice, Statistical Briefing Book. http://ojjdp.ncjrs.gov/ojstatbb/corrections/qa08202.asp?qaDate =2006 (accessed December 31, 2009).

p. 75, "Gang members are involved in . . . ": U.S. Department of Justice, "Juvenile Offenders and Victims: 2006 National Report," Office of Juvenile Justice and Delinquency Prevention, 2006, 84; U.S. Department of Justice, Statistical Briefing Book.

p. 76, "When a case . . . ": "Juvenile Delinquents and the U.S. Supreme Court," 104–106.

p. 77, "Juvenile Delinquents and the U.S. Supreme Court," 100–103.

p. 79, "Juvenile detention facilities vary . . . ": Juvenile Delinquents and the U.S. Supreme Court," 219–223.

p. 79, "Most juveniles in residential facilities . . . ": U.S. Deparment of Justice, Statistical Briefing Book.

p. 79, "In Wisconsin, for example . . . ": "Wisconsin Department of Corrections, Juvenile Corrections," www.wi-doc.com/Type1_facilities. htm (accessed December 31, 2009).

p. 80, "Despite efforts by Wisconsin . . . ": Ashley Fantz, "Sex Abuse, Violence Alleged at Teen Jails Across U.S.," CNN.com, 2008, www.cnn.com/2008/CRIME/04/04/juvenile.jails/index.html (accessed July 27, 2010).

p. 80, "Another report by . . . ": "Feds Begin Tracking Sexual Violence in Juvenile Jails," *Contemporary Sexuality* (October 2008), 9.

p. 81, "Inmates who . . . ": Maia Szalavitz, "Why Juvenile Detention Makes Teens Worse," *Time*, August 7, 2009, www.time.com/time/printout/0,8816,1914837,00.html (accessed December 31, 2009).

p. 81, "Juveniles in confinement . . . ": NPREC, National Prison Rape Elimination Commission Report, 2009, 16.

p. 81, "There also have been reports . . . ": Diana Jean Schemo, "Report Recounts Horrors of Youth Boot Camps," *New York Times*, October 11, 2007.

p. 82, "In 2008, reporter Seamus McGraw . . . ": Seamus McGraw, "Teen Boot Camp: A Deadly Decision?" *Reader's Digest* (June 2008).

p. 82, "A study of New York": Nicholas Confessore, "Four Youth Prisons in New York Used Excessive Force," *New York Times*, August 25, 2009.

p. 83, "Approximately 8,500 youths . . . ": NPREC, National Prison Rape Elimination Commission Report.

p. 83, "An increasing number . . . ": Andrew Gumbel, "America Has 2,000 Young Offenders Serving Life Terms in Jail," *Independent*, October 12, 2005.

p. 83, 85, "In 2009, New York State . . . ": Adam Liptak, "Weighing Life in Prison for Youths Who Didn't Kill," *New York Times*, November 7, 2009. www.nytimes.com/2009/11/08/us/08juveniles.html (accessed July 22, 2010).

p. 84, "Mental Health Needs of Juvenile Offenders": Solomon Moore, "Mentally Ill Offenders Stretch the Limits of Juvenile Justice," *New York Times*, August 10, 2009.

p. 85, "Nevertheless, states across America . . . ": Nebraska Juvenile Correctional Facilities Master Plan Update (June 2007): 4–7, 7–8.

p. 85, "For example, Berks County . . . ": Models for Change: Systems Reform in Juvenile Justice, "Reducing The Incarceration of Youth of Color in Berks County, May 13, 2009, http://modelsforchange.net/reform-progress/14 (accessed January 27, 2010).

Chapter 7

p. 86, "Talbot's article relates . . . ": Margaret Talbot, "The Lost Children," *New Yorker*, March 3, 2008, 58–67.

p. 87, "A 2009 report . . . ": The Constitution Project, "Recommendations for Reforming Our Immigration Detention System and Promoting Access to Counsel in Immigration Proceedings," 2009, 1–37.

p. 88, "Living conditions at Hutto . . . ": Talbot, "The Lost Children."

p. 89, "However, unpleasant conditions remain . . . ": The Constitution Project, "Recommendations for Reforming Our Immigration Detention System," 75.

p. 89, "In January 2010 . . . ": Nina Bernstein, "Officials Obscured Truth of Migrant Deaths in Jail," *New York Times*, January 10, 2010.

p. 89, "A 2009 report by . . . ": Human Rights Watch, "US: Immigration Detention Neglects Health," March 17, 2009.

p. 90, "Amnesty International, another organization . . . ": Amnesty International, Jailed without Justice: Immigration Detention in the USA, June 2008, www.amnestyusa.org/uploads/JailedWithoutJustice.pdf (accessed July 27, 2010)

p. 90, "Thousands of those being detained . . . ": Renee Feltz, "A New Migration Policy: Producing Felons for Profit," NACLA Report on the Americas (November/December 2008): 26–29.

p. 90, "At one of these facilities . . . ": Mark Dow, "Designed to Punish: Immigrant Detention and Deportation," *Social Research* (Summer 2007) 542.

p. 93, "U.S. representative Brian Bilbray . . . ": Tori Richards, "Upgrades to Illegal Immigrant Facilities Probed," AOL News, www.aolnews.com/article/proposed-ice-detention-center-upgrades-questioned/19534495 (accessed July 18, 2010).

p. 93, "In 2008, the American Bar . . . ": Julia Preston, "Lawyers Back Creating New Immigration Courts," *New York Times*, February 9, 2010.

p. 93, "*American Jails* reported . . . ": "The Immigrant Inmate: How Do Jails Cope?" *American Jails* (September/October 2008): 5, 93.

p. 93, "The issue of Americans having . . . ": Stephanie Condon, "Alabama Gov. Candidate Tim James: 'We Speak English. If You Want to Live

Here, Learn It'," CBS News, www.cbsnews.com/8301-503544_162-20003524-503544.html (accessed July 27, 2010).

p. 93, "In 2009, President Barack Obama's . . . ": Bernstein, "Officials Obscured Truth of Migrant Deaths in Jail."

p. 94, "Late in 2009, ICE issued . . . ": U.S. Department of Homeland Security, "ICE Detention Reform: Principles and Next Steps," October 6, 2009.

p. 95, "The Government Accountability Office . . . ": United States Government Accountability Office, "Information on Certain Illegal Aliens Arrested in the United States," April 2005, 1–4.

p. 96, "Such moves concerned U.S. representative . . . ": Spencer S. Hsu, "Agency Plans to Improve Oversight of Immigrant Detention," *Washington Post*, August 7, 2009, www.washingtonpost.com/wp-dyn/content/article/2009/08/06/AR2009080601543.html (accessed July 28, 2010).

p. 96, "To deal with the conditions . . . ": Letter to the author from Senator Joseph Lieberman, January 12, 2010.

Chapter 8

p. 97, "Serial killer Gary Ridgway . . . ": "Green River Killer Avoids Death in Plea Deal," CNN.Com, 2003, www.cnn.com/2003/LAW/11/05/green.river.killings (accessed January 13, 2010).

p. 98, "Ridgway is one of . . . ": Ashley Nellis and Ryan King, "No Exit," The Sentencing Project, 2009, 3–39.

p. 98, "Betty Finn does not sympathize . . . ": Gabriel Falcon, "'Lipstick Killer' Behind Bars Since 1946," CNN.com, October 25, 2009, www.cnn.com/2009/CRIME/10/24/illinois.lipstick.murders/index.html (accessed July 14, 2010).

p. 99, "Many lifers are kept in . . . ": Adam Liptak, "To More Inmates, Life Term Means Dying Behind Bars," *New York Times*, October 2, 2005.

p. 100, "Among those serving . . . ": Nellis and King, "No Exit," 3, 6.

p. 101, "As of 2009 . . . ": The Pew Center on the States, One in 31: The Long Reach of American Corrections (March 2009): 1-6.

p. 102, "One analysis in the . . . ": Joel M. Caplan, "Parole System Anomie: Conflicting Models of Casework and Surveillance," Federal Probation (December 2006), www.uscourts.gov/uscourts/FederalCourts/PPS/

Fedprob/2006-12/parolesystem.html (accessed January 11, 2010).

p. 102, "In testimony before . . . ": House Appropriations Subcommittee on Commerce, Justice, and Science, Innovative Prisoner Re-Entry Programs, congressional testimony of Stephen Manley, March 11, 2009.

p. 104, "A 2008 American Public . . . ": Erik Eckholm, "Innovative Courts Give Some Addicts Chance to Straighten Out," *New York Times*, October 15, 2008.

p. 104, "Nevertheless, research showed . . . ": Nicholas Freudenberg et al., "Coming Home from Jail: The Social and Health Consequences of Community Reentry for Women, Male Adolescents, and Their Families and Communities," *American Journal of Public Health* (September 2008).

p. 104, "For example, the Deuel . . . ": Michael Farrell, "Parole Holds Key to California Prison Overcrowding," *Christian Science Monitor*, September 27, 2009.

p. 104, "Amy Solomon, a senior research . . . ": Senate Judiciary Committee, Reducing Recidivism.

pp. 105–106, "A Parolee Program in Washington, D.C.," U.S. House of Representatives Committee on Oversight, The Local Role of the United States Parole Commission, congressional testimony of Adrienne Poteat, September 22, 2009.

Chapter 9

p. 107, "In 1993, Atkins described . . . ": Elaine Woo, "Susan Atkins Dies at 61; Imprisoned Charles Manson Follower," *Los Angeles Times*, September 26, 2009, www.latimes.com/news/obituaries/la-me-susan-atkins26-2009sep26,0,4180642.story?page=1 (accessed December 12, 2010).

p. 107, "At her trial years earlier . . . ": Edecio Martinez, "Susan Atkins Death Peaceful Compared with Sharon Tate's," CBS News.com, September 25, 2009, www.cbsnews.com/8301-504083_162-5339017-504083.html (accessed December 12, 2010).

p. 107, "Her family argued that . . . ": Jim Avila and Felicia Patinkin, "Susan Atkins on Quest for Parole, Forty Years after Charles Manson Murders," ABC News.com, August 7, 2009, http://abcnews.go.com/GMA/MansonMurders/story?id=8240770&page=1 (accessed December 12, 2010).

p. 109, "Even Vincent Bugliosi . . . ": Richard Winton and Hector Becerra, "Manson Follower Susan Atkins Is Denied Parole," *Los Angeles Times*, September 3, 2009, http://articles.latimes.com/2009/sep/03/local/me-susan-atkins3 (accessed December 12, 2010).

p. 109, "Sharon Tate's younger sister . . . ": Martinez, "Susan Atkins Death Peaceful."

p. 109, "Steve Chapman, a noted . . . ": Steve Chapman, "Let Us Ask Whether Their Victims Were Shown Compassion," *Gaston Gazette*, September 28, 2009, www.gastongazette.com/articles/ask-38427-compassion-let.html (accessed December 12, 2010).

p. 109, "In fact, the Federal Bureau . . . ": U.S. Department of Justice, Federal Bureau of Prisons, Compassionate Release; Procedures for Implementation of 18 U.S.C 3582 (c) (1) (A) & 4205 (g), May 19, 1998, www.bop.gov/policy/progstat/5050_046.pdf (accessed December 12, 2010).

p. 110, "In 2009 in California . . . ": Cara Buckley, "Law Has Little Effect on Early Release for Inmates," *New York Times*, January 29, 2010, www.nytimes.com/2010/01/30/nyregion/30parole.html (accessed December 13, 2010).

p. 111, "In her view, criminals gave . . . ": Sasha Abramsky, *American Furies: Crime, Punishment, and Vengeance in the Age of Mass Imprisonment* (Boston: Beacon Press, 2007), 59–63.

p. 111, "Ted Deeds of the . . . ": Iver Peterson, "Cutting Down on Amenities To Achieve No-Frills Jails, *New York Times*, July 10, 1995, www.nytimes.com/1995/07/10/nyregion/cutting-down-on-amenities-to-achieve-no-frills-jails.html?pagewanted=2 (accessed December 18, 2010).

p. 111, "In Shehane's home state of . . . ": Marty Roney, "36 States Release Ill or Dying Inmates," *USA Today*, August 14, 2008, www.usatoday.com/news/nation/2008-08-13-furloughs_N.htm (accessed December 13, 2010).

p. 112, "In September 2010 . . . ": Pew Center on the States, National Research of Public Attitudes on Crime and Punishment (September 2010), www.pewcenteronthestates.org/uploadedFiles/wwwpewcenteronthestatesorg/Initiatives/PSPP/PSPP_National%20Research_web.pdf?n=6608 (accessed December 14, 2010).

Chapter 10

p. 114, "Violent crime rates . . . ": Office of Justice Programs, "Bureau of Justice Statistics," http://bjs.ojp.usdoj.gov/index.cfm?ty=tp&tid=3 (accessed January 18, 2010).

p. 115, "In the state of Louisiana . . . ": American Civil Liberties Union of Louisiana, "Prison Reform," www.laaclu.org/page.php?id=39 (accessed January 15, 2010).

p. 115, "Outside Los Angeles, in Lancaster . . . ": Joe Domanick, "Anatomy of a Prison," *Los Angeles Magazine* (September 2009).

p. 115, "In Alabama, the state . . . ": Kirk Johnson, What to Do about the Prison Problem? The Pros and Cons of Privatized Prisons in Alabama, Alabama Policy Institute, 2006.

p. 116, "Meanwhile, other states . . . ": Cindy Horswell, "Texas Cuts Costs Amid Prison Reform," *Houston Chronicle*, December 15, 2009.

p. 116, "In 2008, New Mexico governor . . . ": John Bigelow, "Increasing Public Safety in New Mexico before, during and after Incarceration: New Directions for Reform in New Mexico Corrections," Governor Richardson's Task Force on Prison Reform, 2008.

p. 117, "In recent years, the state . . . ": Brian Fischer, "A Model for Prison Reform," *New York Times*, January 5, 2010.

p. 117, "Georgia has faced . . . ": A. J. Sabree, "Georgia Reentry: A Transformation in Correctional Philosophy," *Corrections Today* (December 2007).

p. 119, "A Restitution Program,": Helen Epstein, "America's Prisons: Is There Hope?" *New York Review of Books*, June 11, 2009, 30–31.

Further Information

Books

Edge, Laura. *Locked Up: A History of the U.S. Prison System.* New York: Twenty-First Century Books, 2009.

Hanrahan, Clare. *America's Prisons.* New York: Greenhaven, 2006.

Jacobs, Thomas A. *Teens Take It to Court: Young People Who Challenged the Law—and Changed Your Life.* Minneapolis, MN: Free Spirit Publishing, 2006.

Smith, Lisa, and Linda Wagner and John Aarons. *Dispatches from Juvenile Hall: Fixing a Failing System.* New York: Penguin, 2009.

Websites

National Institute of Justice
www.ojp.usdoj.gov/nij

Office of Juvenile Justice and Delinquency Prevention
www.ojjdp.gov

U.S. Department of Justice—Office of Justice Programs
www.ojp.usdoj.gov

U.S. Immigration and Customs Enforcement
www.ice.gov

Bibliography

The American Prison. New York: The American Correctional Association, 1983.

Muraskin, Roslyn, ed. *Key Correctional Issues.* Upper Saddle River, NJ: Pearson/Prentice Hall, 2005.

Myers, David. *Boys among Men: Trying and Sentencing Juveniles as Adults.* New York: Praeger, 2005.

Schwartz, Sunny, and David Boodell. *Dreams from the Monster Factory: A Tale of Prison, Redemption and One Woman's Fight To Restore Justice to All.* New York: Scribner, 2009.

Index

Page numbers in **boldface** are illustrations and photographs.

About the Author

JEFF BURLINGAME is the award-winning author of roughly twenty books, including *The Lost Boys of Sudan* in our Great Escapes series. In 2011, his book on Malcolm X was nominated for an NAACP Image Award for Outstanding Literary Work—Youth and Teens. Before becoming a full-time author, Burlingame was a writer and an editor for various newspapers and magazines. His most recent books for Marshall Cavendish Benchmark are *The Titanic Tragedy* in the Perspectives On series and *Government Entitlements*, in this series. He resides with his family in Washington State.